# NOBODY ELSE WILL LISTEN

## BOOKS BY MARJORIE HOLMES

LOVE AND LAUGHTER
WORLD BY THE TAIL
TEN O'CLOCK SCHOLAR
SATURDAY NIGHT
CHERRY BLOSSOM PRINCESS
FOLLOW YOUR DREAM
SENIOR TRIP
LOVE IS A HOPSCOTCH THING
WRITING THE CREATIVE ARTICLE
TO TREASURE OUR DAYS
I'VE GOT TO TALK TO SOMEBODY, GOD
WHO AM I, GOD?
TWO FROM GALILEE
NOBODY ELSE WILL LISTEN

# NOBODY ELSE WILL LISTEN

# A Girl's Conversations With God

MARJORIE HOLMES



DOUBLEDAY & COMPANY, INC.
GARDEN CITY, NEW YORK, 1973

ISBN: 0-385-04458-5
LIBRARY OF CONGRESS CATALOG CARD NUMBER 72-84919

PRINTED IN THE UNITED STATES OF AMERICA
FIRST EDITION

*For* MICKIE *and* MELANIE

LISA *and* KAREN

KATHY *and* SUSETTE

# CONTENTS

# NOBODY ELSE WILL LISTEN

## NOBODY ELSE WILL LISTEN

Forgive me, Lord, but I'm turning to you because nobody else will listen. Almost nobody else will listen.

Parents try to but they can't. Most of the time they can't. So often they're not even around when I need them. Or they're too busy with their own affairs to listen. Or maybe they're scared to listen.

My friends and I talk, we talk a lot, but they've got their own problems. None of them really listens.

I prayed when I was just a little kid, God, prayers I'd been taught. It was all very innocent and simple, like talking to Santa Claus. Well, I'm not so innocent any more and it isn't simple any more. It's real, very real, my need to talk to—someone. To seek help somewhere. And even if I never see you, never hear an answer, I know that you too are real.

Now that I'm older I'm beginning to feel it, deep inside. Where it helps and where the very wonder of it hurts sometimes. You made the universe, you made the world. You made *me*. Me, with all these hopes and dreams and faults.

*You are listening*. Day and night you are with me, listening.

I can tell you how it is, in my own words now. You won't criticize, you won't be shocked. You will listen.

Thank you for listening to me, God.

## WHY AM I SUCH A MESS?

Sometimes it seems nobody loves me, Lord. And to be quite frank I don't see how they can.

I am so clumsy so much of the time. My hair looks awful, I'm having trouble with my skin. I eat too much, I often stuff myself until I am ashamed. I say and do stupid things.

I cry for no good reason. I lash out at people. I feel sorry for myself.

Oh, God, why am I such a mess?

Please listen to my cry of despair and help me, help me. Make me tall and proud with life. Let me think of you supporting me, actually supporting me so that I'll stand up straighter.

Let me think of you, a healing, cleansing force that will wash my skin problems away and make my hair smooth and shining. Let me think of you filling me with so much joy and love that I won't need to keep raiding the refrigerator.

Lord, let me remember that no miracle is beyond you if I will just relax and stop fighting life the way I do.

With you I will laugh more, sing more, talk more brightly, or just keep a peaceful silence. I'll remember that nobody's out to hurt my feelings—they aren't that important! That nobody can hurt me half as much as I've been hurting myself.

Thank you, dear Lord, for not despising me even though I'm such a mess. Thank you for loving me and helping me to become a more lovable person.

## DON'T LET ME BE SO CRITICAL

Don't let me be so critical, God.

It seems as if I can find something wrong with everybody. My folks, my friends, my teachers, the kids at school. Every time I see anyone it's as if a little computer starts clicking away in my brain, feeding me their faults.

Filing them away for future reference with which to remind myself: "He's not so great . . . She's not so much."

Help me to stop doing this, God.

It doesn't build me up, make me any better. It only drags me down to something mean and negative, that makes me worse than anybody.

Help me not to be so critical, not to hoard faults.

Help me to smash this computer of criticism, Lord. Let me replace it with one that seeks the good in other people.

A machine that's quick to pick up things to admire. Traits to like, to applaud. Help me to assemble in my mind a file of love.

For whatever I look for I'll find, and whatever I hold inside myself I'll become.

Thank you for showing me this, Lord.

## THE DANCE

Go with me to this dance, God.

I'm so happy to be going . . . but so nervous.

Let the happiness prevail and show. Let it flood away the fear. Let the happiness make me relaxed, so filled with the sheer joy of life that I can let go and really dance!

Please let the boys realize this so they'll ask me to dance with them. But no matter what happens, let me be glad to be there. Glad just to hear the music and mingle with the crowd. And able to share my gladness with others—especially girls who may be even more nervous than I am. (Correction—*was!*)

And the boys too, God. Let this honest gladness, inside as well as out, put them at ease too. Even the ones I don't care for. And when a boy I really like dances with me (please, Lord, let there be at least one), help me just to be myself, but so friendly and enjoyable he'll want to ask me again.

Thank you that I can talk to you about this dance.

You've given me confidence, God. And it's so comforting to know there's nothing too trivial to pray for.

## JEALOUSY

Please, God, help me to overcome jealousy.

It's like a sickness, it torments me, and yet there is an awful fascination about it too. I almost crave the pain and that's what scares me. I've got to get rid of it, God, or my life will be ruined.

I'm jealous of my sister, all the attention she gets, her popularity. I'm jealous of my friends, I don't want them to like each other, only me. And this boy—I'm so jealous of him I could die.

I know that's why I lost him. I was so scared, so suspicious and possessive I made us both miserable. And now that he's dropped me for another girl my heart is stabbed. When I see them together I feel choked, my voice shakes—and my knees. I do stupid things, I talk and laugh too loud to call attention to myself. Or I sulk, knowing my bitterness is showing in my eyes.

Don't let me be like this, Lord. I hate it in myself and know it makes me hateful to others. It's driving away the very people I want to love me!

Cure me of this ugly sickness, please. Maybe just confessing it will help me to understand it better, be the first step toward being free.

Is it because I don't like myself enough to think that other people can really like me? Is that why I'm so scared of losing them, Lord, because I feel unworthy? Whatever it is, help me to get over it, starting now. Give me a cheerful, healthy self-respect so strong I won't have to stoop to jealousy.

I feel better already. I feel relieved, reborn, almost gay.

Thank you for freeing me, I hope forever, from jealousy.

## THE LONELY EVENING

Help me to get through this evening, Lord. This terrible evening.

I'm all alone and I've never known what it was like to be all alone before. Not just alone in the house but alone inside. Alone in my heart, in my spirit.

Nobody wants me, everybody's too busy for me. Everybody I've called has got something else to do. The girls have all got dates or they're going places with each other and they didn't invite me.

I feel abandoned, God, and it's frightening. I feel like

this house, this silent empty house. There is a great aching, frightening vacancy in me.

Stay by me, God, don't let me panic. Calm me down and comfort me.

I'll turn on some music so it won't be so quiet; I'll get myself something to eat. And I'll think of somebody else to call. There must be plenty of people who are lonely as I am. Kids who'd like to come over, or maybe just talk.

Or even somebody older who's sick or needs somebody. Somebody I could really help get through *their* terrible evening.

Thanks for reminding me I'm not the only one, God. And loneliness is no disgrace.

I'm going to make a new friend, or be a friend to somebody who needs a friend! I'm going to learn something, gain something from this evening.

## SELF-PITY

Lord, please help me to stop feeling so sorry for myself.

I hate it, I hate it. I hate it in other people and I absolutely detest it in me. Yet hardly a day goes by that something inside me isn't whispering and whimpering about poor me. How bad I have things, how much less than other kids. How awful everybody treats me, how unfair my parents are.

Whenever things go wrong this little voice blames them, it's all their fault. Oh, why is life so cruel, why does everybody pick on me?

The voice is lying, Lord, I know it's lying, so why do I listen? Why do I even encourage it sometimes when it only multiplies my misery?

Thank you for giving me the courage to tell it to shut up! To laugh in its face. Actually laugh the next time I hear it counting up my woes.

Next time, if necessary, I'll even sit down and write out a list of the things I've got *going* for me. Things I've got to be thankful for. Then order a new voice for me.

Please give me that new voice, God. A voice that will erase my doleful look and replace it with a smile. A voice so glad and grateful it will drown out the sick voice of self-pity.

(Come to think of it—if that's the voice I hear maybe I'll have less to feel sorry for myself *about!*)

## I GET SO DISCOURAGED WITH MYSELF

I get so discouraged about myself sometimes, God.

All these faults. I keep trying to correct them, but just when I think I've got some of them licked, a couple of new ones, worse ones sometimes, pop up.

Or I'll do or say something I thought I never would again. I'm shocked at myself, I could kick myself. Won't I ever *learn?*

Please be patient with me, God. And help me to be more patient with myself.

I'm trying, really trying to be a better person. Knowing you still love me despite these faults and setbacks helps a lot.

Help me not to get too discouraged with myself.

## THEY ALL DON'T HAVE TO LIKE YOU

Okay, God, I've got to face it: This boy just doesn't like me, and I doubt if he ever will.

I know several girls don't like me. And there's one teacher who sure doesn't like me. No matter how I try to please her, she's down on me for some reason and I've just got to make the best of it.

That's the hard part. Accepting any of this when I don't know *why*. I'm nice to everybody, or try to be. I'm friendly. I'm not perfect, far from it, but I've overcome plenty of faults and I can feel myself improving as a personality.

Then how come everybody doesn't like me, Lord?

I've been taught that if you're just nice to people—without putting on a big act or being a pest—they would. Well, they don't. It helps, but they don't, not everybody.

I might as well face the fact: There are always going to be some people in life who don't like me. (Poor things, just think what they'll miss!) But then I don't like everybody either.

So thank you that I have as many friends as I do. And help me to go on being nice to people. Not for selfish reasons, with the idea of nailing them down as friends. But just because it makes us all feel better.

I'm glad life doesn't have to be a numbers game of friends.

## INVENTORY

I can feel myself getting nicer, God, and it feels so good.

I smile more often, laugh and sing more often. I put myself out to help people more often.

I say nice things to people more often. Things I used to be too shy to say, or that I'd be afraid might give them some advantage. Like when a girl's hair looks great, or some boy has said he likes her, or I hope she'll get a part in the play.

I'm even nicer to my family!

Don't start ordering a halo for me yet, Lord. I've got so many faults, I've still got such a long way to go. But I'm *on* my way, that's the main thing. I'm headed in the right direction toward being a nicer person.

And since I've bemoaned my faults so often, asked you for help so often, I want to thank you.

I hadn't realized it would feel so good.

## THE JOY OF BEING ME

Thank you, God, for the joy of being me, in spite of all my faults.

I'm not as pretty as I'd like to be, not as witty, not as smart. I do so many things I disapprove of and make so many mistakes I sometimes think I'm hopeless.

And yet . . . and yet I sort of like myself.

I like this body you gave me. I've even gotten fond of my face. (What a miracle to look in the mirror and realize it's *me,* really me, looking back!)

A sense of wonder overcomes me sometimes.

Sheer amazement that I'm alive at all, able to look around and see other people, talk to them, fight with them, love them. Able to laugh or to cry, to be happy, to be hurt.

Hard as things often are, God, I wouldn't want to be anybody else. Whatever pains and problems I have they're no worse than anybody else's and they're mine, they're mine!

And all the good things that happen to me too. How could anybody else appreciate them the way I do, enjoy them so much? I'm so grateful sometimes, God, I want to shout and dance and sing. Grateful just for being myself.

Thank you, Lord, for the joy of being me.

## FOR ALL THE PEOPLE

Thank you for my friends, God. And thank you for my family. Thank you for all the people whose lives mingle with mine. Sometimes so frantically, causing so many problems, but sometimes so joyfully, wonderfully too.

Sometimes, for no good reason, my heart just fills up with love for them. I want to hug them, tell them, show them, stage a kind of one-dame love demonstration!

I don't, because I don't want them to think I'm crazy. Yet the sense of love and wonder and gratefulness is almost too much to hold.

Since I complain about them so often, bring problems about them to you so often, I think I'll just tell you.

Thank you, God, for all these people.

# PARENTS

## THEY MAKE ME FEEL SO GUILTY

My parents make me feel so guilty, God.

Even when I haven't done anything wrong, there is this awful feeling in me that they think I have. Or that I might.

And they make me feel guilty about things I neglect. Cleaning up my room, helping around the house. Practicing, homework. Guilty of not being grateful enough for my clothes and my home, the things they give me and the things they do for me.

I *am* grateful, God, even if I don't show it. I do try to help, but I admit I'm selfish and there's never enough time. It's hard to keep up with everything at school and the outside stuff besides; I try to, but I can't practice or study every spare minute. I've got to have some life too, and I feel bad enough already about getting behind.

I'm no angel, you know that, but I'm not all bad. I'm really struggling to make the right decisions, do the right things in a crazy world where it's not easy to tell right from wrong.

Please, God, help my folks to have a little more faith in me. To let me know they trust me and believe in me.

Sure, there are plenty of times when I do things I'm ashamed of, and don't do things I should. Times when I *should* feel guilty. Please help me to do better. But please don't let me feel so guilty about so many things so much of the time.

It's hard to love and be close to parents who make you feel so guilty.

## I'M GLAD THEY'RE NOT PREJUDICED

I'm glad my parents aren't prejudiced, God.

That I can have all kinds of friends, bring all kinds of people home. That skin color or religion doesn't matter, or whether or not somebody's family is richer or poorer than ours. They really believe we're all created equal; they've taught us it's not what somebody looks like or where he comes from that counts, only what he is himself, and how he acts.

Some kids aren't so lucky, Lord.

Some kids' parents brainwash them so they're as prejudiced as they are, or worse. (They're the ones that cause the trouble at school.) And some of my friends are embarrassed at how their parents treat anybody whose background is different from their own.

These kids would like to break away from the blind stupidity of prejudice; its injustice makes them mad. But when they do they have to fight a big battle at home.

Thank you that my parents are more decent, have more sense. That they make everybody welcome. (Sometimes the more different people are, the more interesting they seem to find them.)

I know that when it comes to marrying, they hope I won't

choose anybody *too* different from us. But only because it's hard enough for two people of the same background to make it, let alone adding the complications of race or religion too.

Anyway, I'm glad my parents aren't prejudiced, God. That they've taught us we are all your children.

## I'M SO WORRIED ABOUT MY PARENTS

I'm so worried about my parents, Lord. My mother's health, my father's job. They don't seem to get much pleasure out of life. They're both always so tired, so concerned with problems.

Problems with us kids. Problems with neighbors, the things they belong to, the people they work with. Problems with the car. Problems with bills—there's never enough money to go around.

I lie awake sometimes worrying about their problems. I feel so frustrated, God. As if I've got to rush out and get hold of some money to help them. Find it, win it. (A beauty contest? Fat chance! The prize money on a TV show?) I even consider quitting school to go to work. Only they'd be horrified; they wouldn't let me.

I want to say something to encourage them, comfort them. But I feel so helpless about this too. What right have I to try to advise them? I don't know enough. And I don't know what it is they're trying to find in life, what it is they want. (I'm not sure they know themselves.)

So I guess all I can do is try to keep the problems I cause them at a minimum. And to help more around the house, not get so mad at Dad. Not keep asking for things they can't afford. To keep up my grades. To earn what money I can part time and not blow it foolishly. To pray for them and let them know I love them.

It's a pretty large order, Lord, so I'm going to need your help. But thank you for showing me these are some of the things I can do for them.

## WHO'S THE PHONIEST?

These kids drive to school in their parents' cars and spend their parents' money. Some of them spend it on drinking and drugs and the pill, yet they're claiming how bad and phony their parents are.

I agree there are a lot of phony parents, sure. But when I'm with the kids who are blowing their parents' money at the same time they're running them down, I wonder who's the phoniest.

Help me not to call people names unless I'm sure the names don't apply to me. Help me not to be a phony, Lord.

## I'VE BEEN SO CROSS TO MY PARENTS

I've been so cross to my parents lately, Lord, I can hardly stand myself.

Why am I like this? Everything my mother says, no matter how simple, drives me up the wall. I snap at my dad and slam off sometimes even when he's handing me money or the keys to the car.

Even though I'm grateful there's this awful hostility in me too, as if every conflict we've ever had is still seething just underneath the surface, making sure I don't forget. Or as if a part of me is demanding, "What right have they got to have the money or own the car? What right have they got to tell me what to do?"

My common sense tells me this is crazy. They've earned what they own and I haven't—not yet. (Maybe that's what's bothering me.) And until I'm educated and on my own, of course, they've got some rights; they're responsible for me!

But I don't want to listen to my common sense; I just have this awful urge to be myself, be free.

Please help me to curb it, Lord, at least not take it out on them. They look so bewildered sometimes at the way I've been acting lately; they look so hurt that it hurts *me*.

Thanks for helping me get some of this straight in my mind, God. Don't let me be so impatient. Don't let me be so cross to my parents.

## MOTHER, LET'S MAKE UP

This hurt between my mother and me, Lord, this blind silent misery. I can hardly bear it. I want to run into her arms and ask her forgiveness for the things I've said. I want to tell her how sorry I am, to ask if we can't start over.

But pride holds me back. Pain and resentment hold me back. Until she makes some move to ask my forgiveness for the things *she* said, how can I? How can I?

Lord, help me to do it, please, if only to put an end to this pain that lies like a live thing between us. She's so much older and she's already been through so much; my heart is heavy and sore for *her*.

You know how much we really love each other, in spite of these times when we're apart. Maybe that's why they're so hard on both of us. Thank you for reminding me how much we mean to each other and giving me the courage to tell her so. Right now!

Be with us both as I go to her and say, "Mother, let's make up."

## THEY WANT ME TO BE POPULAR

They want me to be popular, God. They pretend they don't care, but they do.

I can feel my mother's anxiety when the phone doesn't ring or I'm not asked to a party, or have a bad time when I go. Even my dad looks puzzled and let down. And it's bad enough, you know it's hard enough, without that too.

It's so humiliating, Lord. I sometimes put on an act, I even pretend a lot of stuff that didn't really happen so maybe they won't have such—well—contempt for me. Only I mustn't think of it that way, Lord, it hurts too much! I've got to remember they love me and it's my happiness they want. I know they're disappointed for me.

But they're disappointed for themselves too. They want to be proud of me, to brag to other parents, even to worry about me the way other kids' folks do. It worries them more to look at this ugly duckling they've produced and wonder, "How come?"

Please don't let them be so anxious about me, God. Make them realize they're only making things worse for me. They make me more scared than I already am, more tense, so I can't relax and be more fun.

Please make them understand this, God. And give me more understanding of why they're so eager for me to be popular.

## MY PARENTS QUARRELED LAST NIGHT

My parents quarreled last night, Lord, and it hurt, it hurt so bad to hear them. My dad's voice rising, my mother's crying. I stuffed the pillow over my head, but the muffled stab of their quarreling went on, like some bad dream.

I am sore with the memory of it this morning. I can hardly bear to look at them. I feel so sorry for both of them, but I also feel betrayed somehow. I feel let down. As if something I'd always depended on had been ripped away.

How can they be like this, Lord? How could they say such things to each other? My *parents,* who lay down the law for the rest of us. Who are supposed to be so perfect, to know all the answers.

Only they aren't, they don't—that's what shocks me, I guess. To realize that they aren't perfect either. Nobody is.

Oh, Lord, help me not to judge them or add to the misery they must be feeling today. Help me to be nice to them, extra thoughtful, extra kind, and not add to their troubles in any way.

Help me to understand them better, Lord, and don't let me stop believing in them. Let me remember that we all fight with people we love sometimes—and it doesn't mean anything. I fight with my sister. I fight with my brothers. I even fight with the boy I'm going with.

Please, God, help my parents get over their quarrel quickly. And let me keep right on loving and trusting them.

## WHY DO I GET SO MAD AT MY DAD?

Why do I get so mad at my dad, Lord? Why am I so cross to him?

He's a good man, he provides everything I eat and own and wear. He's good to my mother, good to all of us. And he works so hard.

But he bores me, irritates me, almost everything he says and does fills me with impatience, sometimes even contempt. And when he tries to tell me what to do or questions me or criticizes, it's the last straw. I argue, yell, slam doors. And even when he doesn't I'm not really very nice to him.

And I feel guilty about it, God. How can I be this way? How can I do this to him?

Sometimes I see him trudging off lugging his briefcase, or coming in after a hard day and I can hardly stand it. I want to run up and throw my arms around him. I want to tell him I love him and thank him for all he does for us.

But something holds me back. Why, Lord, why?

Please release me from these mixed up feelings about my dad. Forgive me for the way I've treated him, and help me not to be that way any more. Help me to be more kind to him, more patient, more friendly.

I do love him, God, and am grateful to you for him. Please help me to show it, please help me to be nicer to my dad.

## WHEN I'M A MOTHER, WILL I?

Lord, when I'm a mother will I . . .

Try to pick my daughter's boy friends, and always think that those who dress and talk and act the nicest around a girl's parents are the ones you can trust, the ones who'll be best for her? . . .

Want her to be best friends with daughters of *my* friends, and with cousins she can't stand? . . .

Worry when she doesn't have dates, and worry when she *does?* And wait up and ask for explanations when she comes in late?

Lord, when I'm a mother will I tell her how much harder I had things when I was growing up, and what a considerate, generous, helpful, obedient daughter I always was?

Will I forget all the bad parts of being my age now and remember all the good parts and try to mold my daughter into some beautiful memory of myself?

Lord, will I make as many mistakes with my daughter as I think my mother makes with me?

I suppose I will, Lord. But whatever I do, just let me love her as much as I know my mother loves me.

## THE WONDERFUL TALK

Thank you for the wonderful talk I had with my dad tonight. We were so close, Lord, for the first time in years.

He told me a lot of things about himself I hadn't known before, and I was thrilled—and honored. And I was able to tell him things about myself I didn't think I'd dare . . . And he was understanding. He wasn't cross or shocked. He actually seemed to be grateful that I would confide in him.

It was as if you were there too, God, guiding both of us. Listening, leading, guiding. Helping us to understand each other.

The loneliness in my dad seemed to reach out to the loneliness in me, and both of us were surprised to find that it was there.

I don't think we'll ever be quite the same again.

There won't be quite so many barriers between us, quite so many differences. But even if there are, they'll be easier to take.

Thank you for the wonderful talk I had with my dad to-night.

## FOR PARENTS WHO CAN BE COUNTED ON

Thank you, God, that I can always count on my parents. That they will stand by me whenever I need them. And not just for now but as long as I live.

Only lately have I realized this, and it's good to know. It's oh so very good.

I criticize them, complain about them, often resent them, fight with them. But underneath it all is this wonderful knowl-edge—they'll never let me down.

I pray that I'll always be worthy of their loyalty and their love. That I'll be someone they can be proud of, and that I won't add too many complications to their lives.

But I know that no matter what might happen, what trouble

I could get into, or how much I might disappoint them, they can be counted on.

My parents will always come to my rescue. They won't condone anything I do that's wrong, but they will forgive me and they will help me.

They are like you, Lord. They make me realize the wonder of your forgiveness and your love.

# GIRL FRIENDS

❦❦❦❦❦❦❦❦

## THEY DON'T WANT ME

Oh, God, they don't want me, they don't want me.
The invitations are all out now, and I wasn't asked.
They don't like me, they don't want me!

What's the matter with me, Lord? Please tell me, help me. Don't let me go on feeling like such an outcast without knowing why.

Please open my eyes to my own faults. And help me to correct them. Make me more attractive to other people. More at ease. More interesting. More fun.

But help me to see my own qualities too. Don't let this stinging blow blind me to them. Don't let it destroy me. If I give up now and wallow in self-pity I'll never make anything of myself.

Lord, comfort me, help me. You walked with outcasts, and I know you walk with me. So lift me up and brush me off and set me on my way.

Help me to remember that these aren't the only people in

the world. This isn't the only party, the only club . . . I'll find better!

Somewhere there are others who'll accept me, love me, want me. And when I find them, maybe this experience will make me stronger and more ready for them.

Thank you, Lord, for making me realize that the future holds happiness and success for me if I don't give up now.

## I WAS SO UNKIND TONIGHT

Lord, I was cruel to another girl tonight.

She was self-conscious and shy, the way I've often been, but did I help her? No, I patronized her, I showed off, I tried to impress her with how much more popular I think I am.

I used her shyness to make me bold. I used her inexperience to make me seem sophisticated. I did the most contemptible thing there is—I took advantage of her weakness. I even flirted with the boy she was with, not because I liked him but only to impress everybody with how much more attractive I am.

Right now, Lord, I can hardly stand myself. I don't see how you can stand me either; how anybody can.

Please forgive me. I may never see this girl again. But if I do, help me to make up for tonight. And if I don't, let me cancel it out, if possible, by being kind to somebody else like her. Oh, extra kind.

Help me never to be like that again.

## HELP MY FAT FRIEND

Please, Lord, help my fat friend.

Everybody likes her so much; she's so jolly, such a good sport. But underneath that laughing front she's hurt, she's grieving inside.

Boys kid her and have fun with her but they never ask her out. It's even hard for her girl friends to know what to do about her when we're having dances or mixed parties.

The poor kid eats eats eats. She keeps trying diets but she just can't seem to stick with them. She's tried pills too, but they were making her nervous, doing her harm.

We've tried to help her, scolded her, encouraged her, pleaded with her until she's getting a little edgy about it. It's beginning to make her mad.

Only you can help her, Lord. She's got to have a strength beyond her own. A will power beyond her own.

I'm going to start praying for her every day, just as if she was sick (in a way she is, Lord), and ask you for healing. Heal her of her craving for food, put a stronger craving in her to have a beautiful healthy body. To be slim, to have dates, to have fun, find love.

Bless her, Lord. Thank you for helping my fat friend.

## THE MIRACULOUS WORD

This miraculous word, *bless.*

I've been told that there's great power in it, Lord—a strange mystical power. And I've tried it, and it works!

Just to ask a blessing for someone makes me feel better, for some reason—and does good. Just why or how I don't know, but it does.

We can send out help to people we care about. We can bless and help a casual stranger. Even our enemies respond to blessings!

That's the hardest part. I thought I couldn't do it, Lord. Even though you commanded us to do it, I thought, "Oh, no, not me." But then I decided to test it, with the one girl I can't stand.

Every time I've thought of her and begun to hate her, I've made myself ask you to bless her instead. Whenever I see her I've been smiling at her and whispering inside, "Bless her, bless her." I've even urged you to issue a blanket blessing over our big problem, the showdown we were going to have.

And now I can thank you, Lord, that the miracle is happening! She's so much nicer to me. I can see her changing. And our problem seems to be just melting away, resolving itself without a big hassle.

I'll never really like her, but she's not all that bad. I'm beginning to understand her . . . and love her! Instead of all that darkness in my heart about her, I feel shining.

Thank you that I've discovered the secret of this marvelous word *bless*.

## I'M SO ENVIOUS OF THIS GIRL

Please help me to stop envying this girl, God.

Her money, her horse, her clothes, her family, her car. Why *shouldn't* she be popular, I think, with all that going for her? Boy friends, girl friends, no wonder!

But it's more than that I've got to admit. She's got personality, she's got looks, she's got talent. You can't buy things like that; they just *are*.

And she's got them, Lord, she's got everything. And sometimes, forgive me, it simply doesn't seem *fair*.

And now, having gotten it off my chest, please give me some cure for my envy.

If I must make comparisons (I'm afraid there's no cure for that), I'd better start comparing myself with kids who have less. So I'm not the richest, brightest, most popular girl in school, but I'm not the worst off either. There are plenty who'd trade places with me in a minute, who may be envying *me*.

Instead of envying this girl or anybody, Lord, help me to remember my blessings. Remind me to thank you for them instead of yelling, "No fair!"

And though it's hard to do, while I'm at it I'll try to be glad that she *is* so lucky, and ask you to bless her.

It works! Dear Lord, it works.

I feel suddenly better about her, and about myself. I don't feel resentful any more, I just feel glad for both of us!

## I TOLD THIS GIRL TOO MUCH

Oh, God, I told this girl too much.

I confided something I shouldn't have, and now she's spreading it all over school.

They're laughing at me, Lord; I cringe at what they must be saying. I can hardly face anybody.

As for her, I think I hate her. I trusted her and she betrayed me. How could she, how *could* she?

And I hate myself. Me and my mouth! *How could I, either?* My secret, my precious secret—that I could share it with anybody, especially her. I betrayed it too, I betrayed *myself*.

Please, Lord, rescue me from this misery, this torment. Show me what to do.

Hating myself won't help. Just let me learn my lesson, not to be such a fool next time—and forgive myself.

And hating her won't help. It will only aggravate the bitterness . . . Please let me love her, Lord, impossible though that seems. Love her enough to forgive her. And tell her so!

People who know, who've tried it, say love is the great healer. And the greatest power of all.

I'm going to try it, Lord. Please help me.

(And after this help me to keep my big mouth shut!)

## I THOUGHT THIS GIRL HAD EVERYTHING

I thought this girl had everything, Lord. I envied her, remember?

Now I discover that she hasn't got everything, after all. (Nobody has, I guess.) Her dad's an alcoholic, her brother's on drugs. There's been a big blowup in their family, even a scandal about their money. She may have to give up a lot of things.

When I heard this, Lord (I've got to confess, though I'm ashamed to), something terrible happened to me inside. A terrible happiness hit me. As if some devil leaped up yelling, "Great! That helps to even the score."

And I realize now that it's not enough just to stop envying people on the surface; you've got to love them, really love them all the way. And want only good things for them, as much as for yourself.

This is a lot harder than I thought. It's easy to love people who are poorer—they're no threat, people you feel sorry for. But you've got to be a really big person not to gloat over the downfall of somebody you've considered richer, luckier, somebody you've always envied.

Please make me a bigger person, God.

Fill my heart with compassion, enough to cancel out all the envy I felt. Give me genuine love for this girl. And if there is any way I can possibly help her, show me.

Meanwhile, bless her. Help her and comfort her.

## MY FRIEND IS MISSING

My friend is missing, God.

She did it, she did it—she's gone! She's been talking about it for weeks, but we thought she was bluffing, we didn't think she'd have the nerve. But now she's disappeared and that must be it—she's run away . . .

Yet has she? How can we be sure? The papers are full of terrible things that have happened to girls just waiting for a bus, or walking home from school. She could have been kidnaped, she could have been killed.

Oh, God, I'm so scared. I'm so worried. And if I feel this

way, what must her folks be feeling? And what can I do about all this?

Please, God, guide me—should I go to them and tell them what she's been saying? Give them the few clues I have? I don't want to betray her; she made us promise we wouldn't tell.

But those awful things can happen, do happen so often to runaway girls. What's really right? What's best?

Please, God, show me.

And please take care of my friend. Stay close to her, protect her, keep her safe, wherever she is.

## SHE'S PREGNANT

She's pregnant, God. My friend is almost three months pregnant and she doesn't know what to do.

They're too young to get married and the boy doesn't want to anyway; he's already dropped her for another girl. That's one of the worst parts of it; she thought he loved her and now he couldn't care less.

He told her to get an abortion. But how? She hasn't got the money, and she's scared of what might happen. She's desperately scared of so many things.

Scared to tell her parents. They'll die—they trusted her, were always so proud of her.

But she's got to tell them, or somebody, soon. She's got to have help. That's why I'm turning to you.

Give me some answers for her, God.

First, though, just bless my friend and make her realize that you forgive her, you still love her. (She needs love right now so bad.)

And bless her parents and flood them with love and understanding and forgiveness too.

And though it's hard to ask it, bless even the guy that got her into this. (*He* sure needs love and forgiveness even if he doesn't know it. And just by praying for him everybody will be helped somehow.)

Next, give my friend the courage to go to her parents. And give them the courage to take it. (That love I asked for, Lord, all that love!) And show them what's best to do.

Or maybe she should go to a minister first, or a doctor, somebody kind who's been through this often and can guide her, maybe help in breaking the news. Anyway, bless everybody who'll be involved and I know we'll find the answers.

With your help we'll find the answers.

(Help me to learn something from this, Lord.

In spite of the pill, and books and songs and movies claiming sex is so natural and great and should be free, it still creates babies. And terrible trouble when you're not married—terrible fear and shame.

Don't let me bring this kind of trouble on anybody, God.)

## WHY ARE GIRLS SO CATTY?

Why are girls so catty, Lord? Why am *I* so catty?

Why do we have this need to tear each other down?

I promise myself I won't, and after I do it I hate myself. Yet when I'm with someone, I'm as bad as anybody else. And it's not just people I don't like that I attack; sometimes it's my own friends.

Why do I do this, Lord? Why do any of us want to talk about other girls behind their backs? Why do we have this awful desire to do it and get such pleasure from it?

Is it because there's so much competition, and we think that by tearing down somebody else we're somehow building up ourselves?

I know this is wrong, Lord, all wrong.

Actually we're *hurting ourselves*. Showing our meanness, our jealousy, our fear. And boys hate us for it when they find out, boys detest it.

And so much damage is done if it gets back to the girl we've talked about. And it does, it does too often. (There's always somebody who not only cats but tells.)

Please, Lord, help me to remember this the next time I'm tempted. Help me to keep still, shut up, leave if I have to.

If I don't want to grow into a catty woman I've got to cure this habit of being a catty girl now.

## HEART FRIEND

There is nothing in this whole world, Lord, like having one true friend. Just one true, enjoyable, understanding friend.

You know how long I needed one, longed for one, prayed for one. How many times I thought I'd found her. How many times different girls were almost, but not quite, that special friend. (And don't think I'm not grateful for *them*.)

But now it's time to thank you. You answered my prayers. I have my friend.

I recognized her almost from the beginning (maybe because she's so much like me), but I wanted to be sure. And in all the months we've been going around together—well, she's even greater than I thought!

We speak the same language, Lord. Laugh at the same

things. But she's different enough from me to be interesting. I'd rather be with her than anybody I can think of. (Well, any other *girl*. And even plenty of guys!)

And she's loyal. She'd never do anything to hurt me; she's as thrilled as I am over the good things that happen to me.

My heart knows it, my mind knows it, my whole being knows it: I have my friend.

Thank you for her, God. And make me worthy of this friend.

## THE GIRL THEY DISAPPROVE OF

What do I do about this girl my parents disapprove of, Lord?

They refuse to see her good qualities, only the things they don't like. Well, I don't think she's all that bad. Besides, what right have they to judge? Or to pick my friends?

I know they're thinking of my welfare, but it makes me mad. It makes me out so immature or simple-minded that I can't decide for myself. It makes me want to defend her, see her all the more. It makes me mad.

My friend knows how they feel about her and she says okay, so she won't come to a place where she isn't welcome, but there's no reason I shouldn't go around with her if I want.

She tells me I shouldn't be such a baby, let them run my life. If I'm ever going to grow up I've got to do what I please with the people I please and they shouldn't be so bossy and possessive.

She points out a lot of things wrong with my parents. She

tears them down to me the way they try to tear *her* down to me. And this is tearing *me*.

Please, Lord, give me some guidance. I want to be fair to everybody—to her and to my parents and to myself. I don't want to hurt anybody.

Help me to break up with her if that's what you really want me to do. Or help my parents to accept her and try to understand her.

Now that I've talked to you about it, I know everything is going to work out right for all of us.

## WHAT IF NOBODY GETS THERE IN TIME?

This girl keeps threatening to kill herself, God.

In fact, she's tried it a couple of times. She took too much aspirin once; she cut her wrists, but not very deep. The kids say she's bluffing, she's just doing it to get attention. But I'm worried about her, God—how do we know she's kidding? I don't think she really wants to die, but what if she does it again and nobody gets there in time?

She must be terribly hard up for attention to do such things; she must be awfully lonely and confused and suffering deep inside. Is she crying for help, God, asking for somebody to care more about her?

How can I show her I care? How can I get other people to care and give her the help she needs? Lead me, Lord, guide me.

Meanwhile, bless this girl. I know if she could find you, she'd be okay. Speak to her, please; make her feel your presence. Comfort her, hang onto her, don't let her abandon the life you gave her.

## HER BABY IS SO CUTE

Her baby is so cute, Lord. We used to envy her even if she did have to drop out of school and get married. She and her husband used to look so romantic going home with their arms around each other after he got off from work.

And when the baby came it was so cute . . .

But we don't envy her any more; she's envying us.

We saw her yesterday pushing her baby carriage and she looked kind of sad. Her husband's been running around. She misses the kids, misses dating and just having fun.

She calls us up, she wants to come back, to be one of us again . . . Only she can't, not with a husband, no matter what he does. Not with the baby.

We tried it once just to be nice, we tried to include her. Only it didn't work; everybody was uncomfortable.

Please help her, Lord. Bless her, give her back some of the happiness she thought she was going to find.

And, oh, please guard us. Guard me. Whenever I get fed up with school or just too tempted by some guy, guard me from making her mistake.

Please, God, remind me that once you are a wife and mother, you can't become a girl again.

## CLASS SYSTEM

Why can't we all be just people, God? Why this phony class system?

People dividing up, joining together to lord it over other

people. If you're in, you're in, and if you're out, you're out.

Though sometimes some of the in-people condescend to be nice to you, so that you feel a little bit in—which is almost worse. To want to be in so bad, and yet know how it hurts to be out.

You know how I felt today. Some of the in-kids asked me to join them at their special table. I felt very big; I wanted everybody to notice. But when the girl I often eat with came rushing up and wanted to sit with us I didn't know what to do.

I was so embarrassed. I didn't want to snub her, but I didn't want to hurt my chances with the in-crowd either. And when one of them shooed her away, very insultingly, I just sat there, but my lunch was ruined.

I'm ashamed now, God. Why didn't I say, "Aw, come *on*, if she's not good enough for you I'm not either." (At least *something!*) Why was I such a coward?

You know I want to be somebody, but I don't want to be cruel.

Why this separating sheep from goats? This phony caste system. And not just in school either, all through life. The money you make, the neighborhood you live in, whether you belong to the country club or not.

Don't let me be fooled and influenced by it, Lord. So eager to be in that I forget how it feels to be out. Give me the courage to be kind to everybody, whether or not they "belong."

## WE ALL NEED FRIENDS SO MUCH

We all need friends so much, Lord. Life is so empty without friends.

We need them to talk to and laugh with, and just to *be* with. Life is more fun with friends. We don't feel so alone when we're with a friend. We feel protected, comforted, safe somehow.

But friends can be so awful too. When they hurt us, ignore us, when they can't be depended on. When they betray us.

That's the way I feel right now. Like they're just not worth it; I'd rather go it alone than be let down any more by my friends.

Lord, please take this bitterness out of my heart. Help me to forgive my friends. And help them to forgive me for all the times I've disappointed *them*.

## THE SPARKLING DAY

I've just got to thank you, God, for this glorious day with my friends. It's still spinning and sparkling inside me . . . I want to think about it a while and tell you how it was.

The smack of the snowball on my window this morning and I looked out kind of cross and there they were on horseback! And the fun of cooking breakfast for them—our messy pancakes, and spilling stuff, and laughing. And trying to find my boots and climbing on behind, only we were laughing so hard I almost fell off. And the gallop through the snowy fields to the stable . . .

And the smell of it, Lord, tangy and sweet with hay and horse. And the sound of the clanking oat bucket, the jingle of the harness. And your world like a fairyland, Lord, as we rode through it, under white-furred branches with little glittering veils spilling down.

And deciding to stop at that country store for hot cocoa—and the mad chase when we found my horse had gotten away. (Oh, thank you, thank you, that we caught him, God!) But everything struck us funny; even that struck us funny when it was over; we nearly collapsed with laughing.

And then this long, lazy afternoon together listening to records and acting crazy and talking about boys. And calling up people or people calling us . . . But tonight when some of the guys wanted to come by, to our own surprise we all said no, we just wanted to be together, just girls. And we went to the movies and got to laughing so hard even there, we had to leave.

And I can still feel the laughter inside me, Lord, I can still hear its bright echoes. I feel somehow . . . sparkling! Like the snow. Tired, but warm and glowing.

Warmed by my friends, polished up and shining because of girls. Girl friends. Oh, God, thank you for them. And for this day, this glorious sparkling day.

# BOY FRIENDS

❦❦❦❦❦❦❦❦

## WHY DON'T THEY SEEM TO LIKE ME?

The boys don't seem to like me, Lord. Why don't the boys seem to like me?

I know I'm no Miss Teen-Age America, but I'm not ugly either, and I'm not dumb. And plenty of girls who attract the boys are no prize winners either. So what's the matter with me that the boys don't pay attention to me?

Please show me, Lord, please help me.

I get so uptight when I'm around boys, and they probably feel it. I get so scared I won't measure up.

And when they don't bother with me, when nobody walks with me or carries my books or sits with me at lunch, when nobody asks me out and the phone doesn't ring—I get to despising myself. I think I must be loathsome, that nobody loves me and never will.

I know this is all wrong. You love me, Lord, and you want me to love myself. Because how can anybody else admire me and want to be around me if I have such a low opinion of myself?

Give me more self-confidence, God—starting right now. Thank you.

Help me to relax around boys, starting today. To regard them not as madly desirable objects able to make or break my happiness, but just as people. Ordinary people like me. Thank you.

Help me to be more friendly without falling all over myself to please. Thank you . . . Help me to be more fun, without thinking I've got to strain to entertain.

Help me to stop thinking about *myself* so much. Thank you.

I feel sure that if I thank you in advance, God, I will be able to make these changes that will make me a more likable person. I'll be more likable, not only to the boys, but to myself.

## TELEPHONES

Sometimes I hate telephones, Lord.

Sometimes I wish Alexander Graham Bell had never invented them.

A telephone can be so cruel. Hanging on the wall silent . . . silent . . . so stubbornly silent when you're waiting for a call that doesn't come. Or getting your hopes so high with its bright, thrilling music so that you rush to grab it! . . . Only it isn't him . . . Oh, Lord, the bitter blow of a telephone that finally rings when it isn't *him.*

But I love telephones too.

I think all girls and women love telephones far more than boys do or men. Boys are often abrupt on telephones, like they want to hang up and get it over with. Girls cling to the telephone; we talk talk talk to each other, clinging.

Telephones are our lifelines to each other. And to the boys.

Sometimes I hate telephones, Lord; sometimes I love them. But I never take them for granted.

Of all the inventions in this amazing world they can bring the most disappointment or the most happiness. Especially to me, especially to girls.

Thank you for telephones.

## HOW MUCH CAN I HELP THIS BOY?

I feel so sorry for this boy who's always getting into trouble, God. I want to help him, to try to understand him, be the one who'll inspire him to change.

But my parents are having a fit. They say we're judged by the company we keep; he'll ruin my reputation and cause trouble for me too.

This makes me furious, Lord. I fly to his defense. I remind them that Christ wasn't too good to walk with sinners.

Yet a part of me is secretly scared and confused. A part of me is afraid they might be right. Because—I've got to be honest—I'm terribly attracted to him too.

The very air of trouble and defiance about him lures me. There is a forbidden thrill about him that makes me want to stand up for him and prove how brave I am.

Lord, please help me to sort out my emotions. Show me whether or not I can really help this boy without messing up my life.

## HE THINKS I'M BEAUTIFUL

Oh, Lord, he thinks I'm beautiful! This boy thinks I'm beautiful. At least that's what he says, and when I look in the mirror I think he could be right.

My eyes are shining, my hair is lively and shining too, my smile is suddenly brighter. I'm standing straighter, and I feel—oh, lovely and strangely alluring. I feel graceful. Even my clothes look better on me.

I feel, and suddenly believe I am, some of the things I've always longed to be—at least attractive, worth looking at.

Thank you, Lord, for this awareness of loveliness in myself. I want to be beautiful for him. I *will* be beautiful for him—and for all the other people I'm going to meet in life.

I will be beautiful for this boy and for those other people, yes. But also—for myself. It gives me so much self-confidence, it makes me feel so good. The whole world looks wonderfully different.

Thank you for this transformation. (Help me to hang onto it even if he looks a little closer and changes his mind!) Thank you that for once in my life I am beautiful in somebody's sight.

## SO IN LOVE

I'm so in love, Lord, so in love.

I see his face before me. His voice haunts me. I can hardly think of anything else but him.

I dream of him, imagining wonderful scenes between us. I hear him saying the things I long to hear.

Please let him call me. Let this telephone ring right now. Or let me look up and find him coming toward me on the street.

And if this should happen help me control my emotions. Don't let my voice shake, or my knees. Let me be the kind of girl he wants, gay and sweet and lovely and fun. And good. Oh, God, above all, good.

Sometimes it's hard to be good when you're this much in love. But help me to remember that that's what this boy, or any boy worth loving, really wants.

Not a cheap conquest, a thing he can use, but a person. A real person with standards, a girl who respects herself enough to merit *his* respect.

Let him be that kind of boy, God. And me that kind of girl.

And oh, dear God, please make him call me. It's hard to go on dreaming when you're so in love.

## STOOD UP

He's not coming, he's not coming. I've just got to face it, God. I've been stood up.

Despite all my praying, no car's going to pull in the driveway, the doorbell's not going to ring. It's too late. Even the phone isn't going to ring giving me some excuse.

Not now. Not this late.

*I've been stood up.* And it hurts . . . it hurts . . . it stings.

My pride is riddled as I run at last to my room. I am

trying not to cry as I slam the door. But I am crying, Lord, in my disappointment and shame.

Please help me to stop, to calm down. Don't let me be too bitter as I get ready for bed, hang up my clothes. (I dressed so carefully, took so long . . . but no, I can't bear to remember *that!*)

And if my mother or somebody comes asking questions, trying to console me, don't let me take this out on them . . .

Thanks, God, okay, okay, I feel better now. With your help I'll make it. I realize this isn't the end of the world. I'm not the first girl who's ever been stood up and I won't be the last.

And it doesn't prove there's anything wrong with *me*. It just proves there are people you can't depend on . . . and when we start dealing with the opposite sex there are times when we'll be hurt. Hurt plenty, and for reasons we don't understand.

Thank you for showing me this, God. I think now I can go to sleep.

## WHAT DO THEY REALLY WANT OF US?

What do boys really want of a girl? What do they really want of us, God?

Some girls say all any boy wants of us is sex. I can't believe that, Lord. Yes, the urge is strong, and the stimulation everyplace. The books, the songs, the magazines like *Playboy* —it's as if girls were meant for nothing else.

But boys *do* want something else, I think. Something more. At least some boys. They want a girl's friendship. A girl they can laugh with and dance with and really talk to. A girl they can keep, if not on a pedestal, at least someplace comfortable and safe, where there won't be the guilty complications and confusions of sex. A girl they can respect.

God, please make me that kind of girl. Make me enough of a person to be able to interest and entertain a boy without sex. And if boys can't find me that interesting, that worth seeing, let them go someplace else.

Help me to stick to my principles, God. Give me the will power to wait for boys who'll want me for myself.

## GOING STEADY

He wanted to go steady, God, and I thought I wanted to go steady too. To have somebody to meet in the halls, to sit with at lunch. And it looked so great, not having to worry about whether or not I'd have a date.

But we've tried it a few weeks and I'm sick of him already. Comparing him to some of the guys I might (just might) be dating, I find all sorts of things wrong with him. I wonder what I'm missing, if I wouldn't rather take my chances than be stuck with somebody who gets on my nerves and is so boring.

But I don't want to hurt him, Lord. He seems to need the security of my company even more than I need his. (Maybe that's why he's so possessive.) I still like him in many ways; I'd like to still be his friend.

Please help me with this, Lord. Give me the courage to break up with him, but help me to do it kindly, without wounding his pride too much.

## HELP ME TO FOLLOW MY HEART

Lord, what do I do about this terrific guy that the other kids don't like?

They're jealous of him for one thing—he's good-looking and smart, and there's almost nothing he can't do—play the piano, dance, win prizes, sing. No wonder he's conceited; and he is something of a show-off, he does try to run things.

Yet he's really a great guy too. So much more interesting than most of them, so much more fun to be with. He's surely going places, God; I think you've designed him for great things.

But now, right now, he's having a rough time with the kids. He doesn't quite understand why they don't like him. Or why someone like me is almost scared to go out with him. Because they give me a hard time about him, God.

They attack him, put me on the defensive. And while it makes me furious, I'm anxious about my own standing too.

Please give me more courage, more independence, God. If I really enjoy him (and I do) then let me follow my own heart.

He's got so much to offer, this boy the other kids don't like.

## I'M SO FICKLE

The kids say I'm fickle. How can I be in love with so many boys? And I know it seems crazy, but they're right.

There are so many people to choose from (even if they

don't *know* I'm choosing them or pay any attention to me!) that it sometimes worries me. You've seen me so thrilled or so crushed over first one, then another, and sometimes several all at the same time.

But all this variety is exciting too. I can't help thanking you for making so many interesting, attractive people. So many it's hard to believe that someday I'll have to settle for just one.

I know that will have its advantages; it will probably be wonderful. But meanwhile, if by liking so many I'm being fickle, Lord—well, maybe I'm learning things that will help me to pick him!

Anyhow, it's never dull this way!

## THE MYSTERY, THE ROMANCE

I've just seen that old movie *Gone With the Wind*, and I know now what my mother means when she talks about mystery and romance.

I feel almost cheated, God; I feel I've been missing something. I wish I could feel mysterious and prized. Right now I wish I lived in the days of Scarlett O'Hara with hoop skirts and pantalettes. Or the time of the legends, with knights riding off to battle flying my scarf.

I like clothes that are fun and free, but I'm sometimes sick of being, and seeing other people, sloppy and so exposed.

And all these school sex classes, God. I know they're trying to help us, being so frank, but they're also robbing us of so much of the romance.

I don't want to think of the boys I dream about like that, in all the grim physical details. I hate having my own body diagrammed for them.

And our emotions, God. The feelings we have when we're attracted to each other, when we kiss. Do adults have to analyze and explain all this? (It spoils it somehow to know what my glands are doing, and why!)

My mother didn't know as much about sex as I do, but at least her generation had the fun of finding out a few things for themselves. They had some mystery, some romance.

I know they're only trying to protect us, Lord, keep us "safe." But can't you make them smart enough to teach us without ruining what they had?

## IS THIS THE WAY TO PROVE IT?

I'm crazy about this boy, God, but he says I've got to prove it. He says if I really love him we'll have sex.

Oh, God, is he right? I'm scared. I don't feel ready. I'm scared of the consequences—and above all, it doesn't seem right.

Please help me, God. Help me to know what to say to him, how to act with him. Give me the strength to hang onto my self-respect.

I realize—you make me realize—that if he really loved me he wouldn't ask this. If he really cared about me he wouldn't put me through this torment, ask me to take such a risk. He's only thinking of himself.

He has no more right to demand that I prove my love than I have to demand that he prove his!

As I pray I see this, God. Now please help him to see it. And if he won't, give me the will power to break up with him.

Thank you for helping me through this.

## IS HE TOO OLD FOR ME?

They tell me he's too old for me, Lord. My parents are having a fit. But I can't believe it, I don't want to believe it—I'm so crazy about him.

He's so much more interesting than kids my age. He makes them seem like babies. And he makes me feel older too in some ways, superior to them.

But in some ways I feel young and scared and insecure with him. I don't know quite how to please him, how to talk to him.

My folks have put their foot down. Now that they've found out how old he is, they say I can't go out with him. (And this only makes me want to all the more.)

They say that when a guy that much older goes out with a girl my age he's only looking for one thing. Or that he doesn't feel equal to people his own age. This seems so *unfair*, God. How do they know? What right have they got to judge him?

But I'm sick of all the fighting about it. It hurts us all so much—it even hurts him. Please help us, give us guidance, God.

If they're wrong, make them see it and give in, be nice to him. But if they're right, if he's really too old for me, help me to realize it and accept it. (And help him to accept it.)

Thank you for giving us some answers, God. Thank you for blessing this whole problem so it will turn out best for all of us.

## IF IT'S REALLY OVER

He doesn't love me any more, he doesn't even like me! He never calls, he barely even speaks. And now I hear he's going out with another girl.

What have I done to lose him, God? How can I win him back?

I want to write to him, I want to phone him, I want to find out *why*. It seems I've just got to do something to ease this pain. Even if he tells me it's all over, I couldn't feel any worse.

But my mother warns me that would be a big mistake. I can't go crying after him, forcing him to explain. It would only make him hate me. And she's right. I know she's probably right.

I've got to ignore him, leave him alone, find somebody else.

Give me the strength to do this, God. Give me the will power, yes, and the pride. If it's final, if it's hopeless, help me to get over it without making a fool of myself.

Please send somebody else along to take his place. And next time don't let me make the same mistakes I made with him.

## SEX

Sex . . . this marvelous and yet troubling thing called sex. I've got to talk to you about it, God, it's on my mind so much.

But then everybody else seems to think about it too (sometimes it seems they can't think or talk about much else!)—parents, churches, the people who teach it at school. Not to mention the songs and movies and books—even the magazine ads and TV commercials. And the kids themselves.

Sex, sex, sex.

Yet for all the talk about it, nobody seems to know much about it. Not really—there are all these conflicts: It's right, it's wrong; it's fabulous, it's ordinary, save it, spend it—sex, sex, sex!

The result is not only confusing, it's cheapening, God. I'm turning to you to sort out my own thoughts, to reach some understanding.

You, who created us, created sex. You put this fierce sweet hunger in us.

You gave us this power that creates life. Life, Lord—life itself. We share this power with you!

And you made it the most personal thing anybody can share with anyone else. The most secret, intimate, exciting experience.

Even I can see that anything that important wasn't meant to be cheapened the way we're doing. Used merely to satisfy hunger like a meal, or played with like a toy. Nothing but a toy.

That much at least I know about sex. And surely that's what really matters, that basic, vital truth.

Please keep me reminding me of that truth, God, and guide me. So that I will use this marvelous part of me in the way, and only the way that you would want me to.

## THE FALSE STORY

What am I going to do about this terrible story they're telling? The guys are teasing me; the girls are gossiping. And I haven't *done* anything; it isn't true!

I only had one date with that boy who's supposed to be so wild, and nothing happened. You know that, God, we just had a good time.

He swears he never made any false claims, but he must have or there wouldn't be these stories. Or do people just jump to conclusions because they like to think the worst and see people suffer?

And I *am* suffering. My reputation means so much to me, and I don't know how to fight this. I don't know what to do.

My *reputation* . . . Thank you that I already have a good reputation, because that's what will save me now.

The guys who've been out with me know better. The girls who really know me must surely know better too. And even if they don't, I can't be too damaged if my conscience is clear.

Not inside, not where it counts most. All I ever should be truly concerned about is being able to face myself in the mirror—and to face you.

Thank you that I *can* face you, God. It's a lot of comfort. (But next time help me to be more careful about the kind of boy I go out with!)

## DEATH ISN'T THE ONLY WAY

I have grieved, God, you have seen me suffer. Over the death of a grandparent, my dogs and cats and birds. The unbelievable shock of the death of a friend.

But now comfort me in this grief that is in some ways even worse because I'll have to go on seeing the person I have lost.

Death isn't the only way you can lose someone you love.

## THE MUSICIAN

I can hear him playing the piano . . . hear him practicing now . . . and it's beautiful.

So beautiful it almost hurts, it makes me want to cry. It's as if he's speaking to me, trying to tell me something.

Even when he stops and goes back and runs a scale or takes a passage over, there is something plaintive about it, something that's struggling to be expressed. To say something to me.

Am I falling in love with this boy, God, whose fingers can draw such marvelous sounds out of an instrument? In love with whatever it is inside him that makes him want to play it and make it speak? Speak to me!

Only I know it can't be me. He's older; he doesn't even know I'm alive. (At least he doesn't act that way.) But in his music he's calling out to somebody . . . some girl . . . and I like to think as I stand here listening that by some miracle it could be me.

Anyway, thank you for the thrill of hearing him like this, dreaming of him like this. For the sheer beauty and wonder of music and life and being young, with all the possibilities of love in the air . . .

Like this music . . . this unexpected music . . .

Thank you that I happened along this particular corridor today.

## WHY CAN'T IT LAST?

You know I'm never so happy, Lord, or as nice to people, as when I've just fallen in love.

It's so lovely while it lasts. It's like the night before Christmas, filled with excitement and suspense. It's the bells of Christmas ringing and the stars shining and good will and love sparkling for everybody. It's not just the guy I'm in love with; it's the whole world!

Why doesn't this joy last, Lord? Why must it all settle down to habit and dull routine and being cross and finding fault so soon?

Falling in love is the perfect high and it makes me the almost-perfect person for a little while. If only I could tap the source of this joy and keep it, turn it into something permanently beautiful, so that I'd be as nice to people as I am then.

They're happier. I'm happier.

Help me to remember how it feels, and to love all people anyway, and show it, in the times between.

Your love—your lasting love can help me. Thank you for this most beautiful of all loves.

## HE'S SO HANDSOME IT HURTS

He's so handsome it hurts, Lord.

It really almost hurts to look at him. And I think he knows it, because he's so aloof. He holds himself a little apart, as if he's afraid of being hurt himself by all the girls who think he's so cute, and the boys who resent him. He's kind of bitterly amused.

It must be a burden to be that good-looking, God. Judged only by what people can see. I wonder what he's really thinking, what he's like inside. What he'd like to say.

I wish I could get close enough to find out!

## RESTORE MY SELF-RESPECT

I went a little too far last night, and I'm sorry. I'm ashamed to see my own face in the mirror. Whenever I think of the boy I was with I cringe.

Please don't let him lose all respect for me, Lord. Don't let him think I'm that way with everybody. I don't care what other people do; this isn't right for me and I don't want anybody thinking it is. Thinking I'm easy.

Don't let him think so, God, and please, if you love me, don't, oh don't let him talk about me with other boys.

Give me another chance, God. Please let me do something to restore myself in his eyes—and in my own.

Maybe I'll feel better, now that I've confessed to you, if I do something for somebody else. Help somebody, do something especially kind. Or if I give up something I really want, make some sacrifice.

I'll do whatever it is, anything. Only make me feel right with myself again. That I've got a firm grip on my own ideals again. Ideals that, in a crazy moment, I almost abandoned altogether.

Thank you that I didn't quite, Lord. And give me more strength next time.

Thank you for restoring my self-respect.

## THE BEAUTIFUL HOUR

We walked together, this boy and I, through the windy park. And it was beautiful. So beautiful . . .

We had just met, we didn't even know each other, yet in that hour we came to know each other in a way I've never known anyone before.

He found beauty in so many things, God, and he roused me to their wonder and beauty too. The music of acorns falling, the spicy tang of leaves; the pigeons strutting, their colors shining in the sun.

He knelt and softly called them and they came. We stroked the silky smoothness of their feathers and it all seemed new, excitingly strange and new. Even the ducks on the pond, gliding and quacking and quarreling, seemed comically sweet and new.

A big collie out of nowhere came tagging along. He even jumped in the boat the boy rented to row a little way up the river; the dog sat there very regal with his big gazing eyes . . . We talked about the strangeness of animals, how they can't speak and yet how much they seem to say.

We talked about life. How mysterious it is to live at all. We talked about love and people and values. We talked about you.

And when we came back, with the lights just coming on, we met a ragtag old man playing a harmonica and selling pretzels. And the music was both merry and sad and so was he. (And so were we.)

We bought some and ate them walking back across the park, holding hands.

Mine stuck in my throat for some reason (maybe it was too dry). I crumbled it up and fed it to the pigeons, who looked even lovelier in the falling dusk and the light of those first street lamps.

Another guy came running up then and said their bus was leaving, they'd have to go. (He was just in town for the day.) So suddenly he was gone, and I don't even know his last name.

I'll probably never hear from him, never see him again—and in some ways I don't want to. (Beautiful things have a way of getting spoiled.) But it was wonderful . . . I loved him for a little while and I think I love him now.

Thank you for this beautiful hour, God.

# SCHOOL

## I *WON'T* STAY HOME AGAIN

Please, Lord, give me the courage to get up and go to school today.

I've already been sick so often, or played sick so often, I can hardly stand myself. I'm behind on my work and the longer I stay home the harder it will be to catch up. And the harder it gets to face my mother's anxious, worried eyes.

Lord, Lord, I hate myself. This awful longing just to lie here drowsing, dreaming, pretending that my head aches (though it does a little), that I'm too weak.

Weak-kneed, that's what I am! . . . Oh, Lord, don't let me be such a coward, dreading the classes, the crowds, and having to make my way with the kids. Give me the strength to face it, body strength and strength of character.

Please, Lord, change my dread to anticipation.

Thank you for making me realize that if other people can take it, so can I, and school isn't all that bad. That's where the action is, that's where life is! And even if it's rough I've got to be there or I'll miss it.

With your help I can make it; I *will* make it. I won't drag myself out of this bed, I'll jump out. I'll take a shower, wear something bright to match the day.

Because the day *is* bright—too nice to waste in bed. Thank you for this beautiful day, God, and for the feeling that out there something wonderful is going to happen. Something that couldn't possibly happen if I stayed home sick again.

## HELP ME WITH THIS TEST

Oh, God, make me calm and confident before this test.

Please take the anxiety from me. Help me to stop worrying about the questions I can't answer, and to feel cheerful and grateful for the ones I can.

Help me to remember just to read the whole thing swiftly through and then concentrate on what I really know. Give me correct choices. And the words to express myself. Let me remember the facts I think I've forgotten. But even if I can't, don't let me sit fretting and stewing about it.

Sit beside me, Lord. If you're there I won't be tempted to cheat. I won't feel too badly if I falter or even fail. But with your presence guiding me I'll be able to do my best.

That's all that really matters, so help me to do my best.

Walk with me now into that room, Lord. Be with me through this test.

## THE SUBJECT I HATE

I hate this subject, Lord. Simply hate it.

It's my enemy. It can keep me from passing. It ruins my day—well, a chunk of my day, at school. Every time I go to class it's like being dragged to my doom. I suffer, Lord. I sit blind and angry, scared the teacher will call on me to defend it, be its ally, but how can I when I don't understand it and hate it?

There's no escape from it even at home. It's in the room with me now like an enemy army occupying my desk. This big dull book about it and all the stuff I'm supposed to look up. The references, the notebook I'm supposed to keep. It's waiting for me to attack it and the longer I put it off the stronger it will get.

Be my commanding general, God. Give me the courage to start, and show me how to overcome.

I guess the first thing is to pretend I'm not scared. To force a smile if it kills me and ask you to bless it . . . Bless this subject I hate, Lord, bless these papers and books. Don't let me think of it as an enemy any more, but as a friend. A friend I don't care much about but that I *can* get along with, learn to understand.

Change my emotions from fear and distress to curiosity about it. There *is* something in it for me if I can just find it. Change my resentment to a sense of challenge. Unlock my mind, let understanding flow in.

Thank you for the self-discipline it's going to take. Thank you for the rewards that are going to come. I will benefit by what it has to teach me (even though I can't see it now, I *will*—I promise myself I will). Thank you that in the end I'll gain more from winning over this "enemy" than studying a subject that's easy for me.

So here goes, God.

## EVERYTHING WENT WRONG TODAY

Everything went wrong today, God—I mean everything.

I couldn't find the sweater I wanted to wear, I didn't have time to eat breakfast, and I missed the school bus. Mother was mad because she had to take me and when I got there (late) I'd lost my report and forgotten to bring money for lunch.

She was cross, teachers were cross, and the kids were impossible! Worst of all. The girls ignored me—except when I came up to a bunch that were talking about me; I could feel it. Even my best friend was so horrible to me I ran into the girls' room and cried. And when I saw myself in the mirror I looked so awful I cried some more.

And then coming out (wouldn't you know?) I ran right into the boy I've been crazy about, walking with the one girl I can't stand.

Even when I got home, besides all the homework and having to study for a test, Mom had all this stuff lined up for me to help her with.

It's very late now, God. I'm so tired, forgive me if I don't do anything right now but just thank you that this awful day's over, and that you gave me the strength to get through it.

It's a comfort just to tell you about it. Please let me get a good night's sleep, I know tomorrow will be better.

## REPORT CARDS

Lord, I don't know whether I should thank you or not for this report card.

I prayed so hard it would be a good one. The last one wasn't and I'd hate to go through *that* again. Teachers making threats about getting into college. Mother's disappointment, Dad's yelling. Even his bribe . . . ten dollars for each *A,* five for a *B,* and if I made twenty-five he'd match it.

I bought the deal but it also made me kind of sick. Everybody making a federal case about my grades, but not one person worrying about what I'd *learned.*

(Who can judge what I really know? Who can look into my mind and see what's happening? Tests don't prove it; we all get scared and there's so much cheating. Class doesn't prove it, some kids just can't recite. Homework and notebooks don't prove it—all that junk that they don't even look at lots of times.)

And these past weeks, Lord, working and worrying for just one reason—to escape all that misery (earn all that money). And my stomach in knots before the cards came out, my heart hammering.

For what? For this. Two *A*'s (twenty bucks) I don't really deserve (I'm not that good, I bluffed and played up to the teachers), and a *D* I don't deserve either. (Instead of going down in that subject I should have come up; I'm finally beginning to get it). Plus a *B* and a couple of *C*'s, which mean nothing.

It's discouraging, God. It's phony.

I suppose they've got to have some way to measure us, but please lead them to something that will give a truer picture.

## THE WONDERFUL TEACHER

Thank you, Lord, for this wonderful teacher.

She's human, she's friendly, she's fair. She acts as if she really likes us. She doesn't put up with anything, but she knows her stuff and she expects us to know ours.

And she makes it all seem *interesting*. Not just something we've got to do so shut up, quit stalling, and do it—but that there is something in it, really *in* it for *us*.

For the first time in years I'm realizing that to learn something, really learn and understand something, can be thrilling . . . at least make you feel very good.

Thank you for the encouragement she's given me, God.

She sees things in me even I didn't know I had. She's taught me more than her subject. She's taught me that nothing in life is impossible, not if you really want to do it. And even if I don't live up to her expectations, I'll never be the same.

Lord, I complain about so many of my teachers it's great to be able to thank you for a change. Thank you for this wonderful teacher, God.

## HE WANTS TO QUIT SCHOOL

He's talking about quitting school, God, my boy friend wants to quit school! Don't let him, please don't let him.

I've pleaded and argued with him, but it doesn't seem to

do any good. He's heard all the arguments so often—about how much he'll regret it later—but he's deaf to them. Please, Lord, help me to think of some new ones that will convince him. Or send somebody else who can convince him.

But mainly I just ask you to reach him.

You made him, and you understand him in a way nobody else can. You know the things that bug him—the teachers, his parents, his problems. And you know the things that drive him—not only his resentments, but his impatience, his restlessness.

Love him, Lord, and get through to him in a way I can't. Fill him with so much love that he'll be free of these things. Make him realize we don't solve our problems by running away from them, we only make more.

Give him the will power to stick it out—and oh, shake some sense into him!

I'm turning him over to you, Lord. Thank you for helping him.

## I WISH I HADN'T CHEATED

I wish I hadn't cheated on that test, Lord. I wish I hadn't cheated.

Sure, maybe all the kids cheat, even some of the kids that make the Honor Roll. The teachers practically expect you to. It's a kind of game trying to catch you, but there's no big deal about it if they do. I'll bet a lot of them cheated in college themselves, cheated to get to be teachers.

So why should I feel so guilty about this, God? The test was hard and I've got to pass that course, so I did it and thought I'd feel good about getting by.

Instead, there is this angry sickness in my heart. This—contempt. Contempt for everybody else, but worse, this awful self-contempt.

I'm mad at the system that makes grades so important. Mad at the teacher who made up such a tough test. (I hope she enjoyed it!) Mad at my friends who can do it all the time and not be bothered. (I'm almost mad at you for giving me a conscience like this.)

But blaming other people doesn't take the heat off my own conscience. I'm mad, above all, at *me*.

To think I'd do this to myself, Lord.

Actually, I just played into the hands of the lousy system and that teacher and everything I can't stand, when I did this to myself. Became a cheat.

Words may not mean anything to a lot of people any more but they still mean something to me.

Words like *liar . . . thief . . . cheat.*

And a cheat is the worst of these words because a cheat is all three.

So I cheated myself, God, out of something a lot more important than a grade. And I'm sorry; I'm so ashamed. Please forgive me.

Don't let me cheat again, God. And give me the courage to do whatever I have to do to make amends for today.

## IT'S ALL TOO MUCH

Sometimes I feel I just can't take it any more, Lord; it's all too much.

All these activities I'm in. All these rehearsals. All these committee meetings. All these lessons I've got to go to and practice for . . . And the homework piling up. And the special assignments—the papers and notebooks and book reports.

And the tests—dear Lord, the tests! . . . I'll be up all night studying . . . My head is spinning. My body is tired, my brain is tired. All I want to do right now is get something to eat and plop into bed and sleep . . . sleep for a week.

But I can't, I've got to get at it, keep at it, keep going.

Give me the strength, God. The sheer physical energy to be able to get *through* it, let alone get something out of it. To learn something, achieve something that will help me as a person.

After all, that's why I do it—or somebody makes me do it. Help me to remember that; there's got to be some valid reason, something in all this that's for *me*—not my teachers, not my folks, not the school, but for me myself. It will be more interesting then, more worth doing, and maybe I won't get so uptight about it.

Thanks, Lord, I can feel the tension easing a little bit. With your help I won't be overpowered by all this; I'll have the strength.

But please do something about those teachers too. Let them realize how unreasonable some of their assignments are. At least lead them to some system where they all won't pile everything on us at once.

As for me, Lord, please help me to cut down someplace. When I have a choice, remind me to take on only those things that are really important, that will help me grow as a person.

## I WON, I WON!

I won, I won! Oh, dear Lord, thank you, it's happened, I really won.

I can still hear them making the announcement, still feel my dazed astonishment. Still hear the kids congratulating me. And the people, all the people who seemed to be truly glad for me.

I just want to keep thinking about it, Lord. That first terrific excitement. I just want to live it over and over again, trying to realize it's really happened, to make myself believe it's true. I did it, I was chosen, I won!

Oh, Lord, I'm so grateful . . . oh, Lord, I'm so humble . . . oh, Lord, I'm so scared.

I keep thinking there might be some mistake; maybe I'll wake up or something, it can't be really me. Yet a part of me is shouting in triumph too.

Telling me this is only the beginning, a preview of the future—the glorious, dazzling future and all the wonderful things I'll do.

Please let me believe that, Lord. Really believe that, without letting it go to my head. It's so thrilling to be a winner, but I've got to be careful; the rest of it won't be easy; it will be tough in some ways too . . .

But don't let me think about any of that right now. Here alone in my room let me just dance around and hug myself and marvel and love everybody in the world.

Let me fling open the window and look up at your stars,

your sparkling stars, and thank you . . . Oh, I do thank you, Lord. I won, I won!

## UNFINISHED BOOK

We went to this teacher's funeral today, Lord—she was only twenty-four. I still can't believe it, nobody can. Last week she was in class assigning our book reports. This week she's gone.

The book I checked out of the library lies on my desk. I'd read only the first few chapters. I pick it up in amazement, wondering if I should finish it?

If I can *bear* to?

I wasn't particularly close to this teacher, God, but I feel terribly close to her now. I want to comfort her somehow. This was her first year of teaching. She was going to be married. Now it's all over, the kids she would have taught, the children of her own she might have had.

The book of her life was just getting *good!* Now it's all over. None of us will ever know how it might have turned out.

I'm crying for her, Lord, crying for this loss. And crying —yes, I'm crying for myself.

Please make her happy, wherever she is. And please, oh please, don't let the book of my life be over until I can read it all the way through.

## THE REAL SELF CAN GET LOST

Thank you that I don't feel it's so necessary to be a part of the in-crowd any more, God.

I used to long to be one of them, remember? But now that

I am or could be it just doesn't matter. It seems so empty most of the time, so shallow and almost funny. Everybody trying so hard to be like everybody else, and yet trying to stand out too.

To *be* somebody, to be the most popular one of all. The most important. To be on top.

And it's so sad because in trying to *be* somebody they've *lost* somebody. The most important one of all—themselves. Their own identity.

And they haven't really *got* anybody, no matter how popular they are. Because everybody else is trying so hard for the same thing—to be on top.

Lord, please help me to be an individual, and hang onto my individuality, in or out of a crowd. It's too exhausting trying to be like everybody else, or to get ahead of everybody else! The real self can get lost in the process. And once you've lost your real self how can you find it again?

God, give me enough independence to be myself wherever I am. Don't let me risk it by thinking I've always got to belong, or to be on top.

## COLLEGE

I keep wondering about college, God.

Do I need to go? Do I want to go? And what will I be going for?

Some girls go to get married (at least to find the guy). Some to join a sorority, have fun (though sororities aren't what they used to be, and college today sounds like a lot of work and a lot more serious stuff than fun). And a lot of kids go, girls as much as boys, because a degree is almost a guarantee of more money, a better job.

But if I do go it's got to be for better reasons, God.

I see plenty of people making plenty of money without going to college. Plumbers, carpenters, truck drivers; or just people who are extra clever, extra strong.

And there are plenty of really wise and wonderful people who've never set foot on a campus.

So if I go it's got to be for something else. To find something I couldn't find otherwise, God . . .

To learn things I really want to know. Not for their money value, but for their value just to me. Things like music and books and art, and science and history. And to develop myself as a person, my poise and self-assurance, as well as my understanding and my mind.

If I go to college it ought to be so that I'll get more out of life, and be able to give more.

I've noticed my parents' friends. The ones who've gone to college just seem to know more about more things. And they seem to have more open minds, to be more curious, to read more, think more, and be willing to learn more.

And all this simply makes most of them more interesting, not only to other people, but to themselves. They seldom seem bored, they live more richly enjoyable lives.

I'm asking myself if this is worth the effort, Lord.

Because it's a whole lot easier *not* to go to college. Not to have to study any more, go to class any more, worry about tests. It's a lot easier just to stay home, get married, or get a job.

Whenever I think of college I get a little scared, I begin to make excuses. But then I weigh the advantages and I'm ashamed.

Thank you for giving me guidance about college, God. If I decide I must go let it be for the right reasons. And give me the ability and strength to really get out of college what I'm going for!

# THE FAMILY

## WHY DO I FIGHT WITH MY SISTER?

Why do I fight with my sister, God?

Even though we love each other it's as if we hate each other too. We resent each other, get jealous of each other, try to get ahead of each other.

We argue about things, we fight over clothes. She borrows my stuff without asking and forgets to give it back. Or it comes back messed up, stockings with runs in them, lipstick on my sweaters. But when I do the same thing to her, she gets mad.

Lord, I sometimes think I'll be glad when she leaves. But when she's away for even a weekend, I get lonely for her. I miss even our arguments.

And when we do talk half the night and share stuff and stick up for each other against our parents or other kids, my heart is so full of love for her sometimes I could cry.

You must have had some reason for putting us in the same family, God. Maybe to test us out against each other so we'll be strong enough to defend ourselves, cope with other people later.

Or maybe to learn that it's possible to fight with people and still love them!

Anyway, I do love her, Lord, no matter how much I fight with her. I am thankful for my sister.

## I HEARD MY BROTHER CRYING

Last night I heard my brother crying, Lord. Crying like I've never heard him cry before, not even when we were little kids.

His door was closed, the sound was muffled, but I could hear it and it nearly killed me. I wanted to go in and do or say something to comfort him. But I didn't dare, he would have driven me out.

Lord, I've often thought it hurts so much to be a girl.

The cramps every month. And the hurt of having to wait for a boy to ask you out. Of not being able just to call him up and say, "Please pay attention to me, talk to me, take me somewhere!"

I've always thought boys had it so good.

Now I know that boys hurt too. Last night I suddenly realized how much a boy can suffer. When a girl turns him down. Or leads him on and then makes fun of him. Or goes with him and drops him for somebody else.

Lord, please comfort my brother. Be with him through this, whatever it is, and help him to get over it.

I suppose it's inevitable that I will hurt boys too, some boys. But please don't let me ever do anything that will make a boy cry like that. The way I heard my brother.

## NOBODY ELSE BUT A FAMILY

I heard or read somewhere: "Home is the place where you act the worst and are treated the best." Now I know what it meant.

I had my period and was cross all day to everybody. I snapped at my mother this morning and was just awful to my brother when he asked me to sew a button on his shirt.

Tonight I left the kitchen for my sister to clean up, even though it was my turn. I even ran off with the car and made my dad late to his meeting.

But when I got in, Mother had saved me the last piece of pie. My brother offered to help me with my math, and my sister not only started my tub, she dumped in her best bath salts.

When my dad got home he came in to see how I was feeling and sat on my bed to "cheer me up" with a long-winded story.

Lying here now with a hot-water bottle and a book I feel so—well—comforted. Loved and looked after and forgiven. And it's just so marvelous to know that people I can treat so bad, who see my very worst side, still care about me and treat me so good.

Nobody else but a family would do this, God.

## TAKE CARE OF HER FOR US

The vet says there's nothing more he can do for her, God, she's better off home with us. I'm sitting with her now, holding her paw and wondering if she'll live till morning.

Your stars are shining through the window and pretty soon the moon will be bright. My father keeps telling me to come to bed, but I want her to know I'm near, Lord. I can't leave her to die alone. (She would never leave one of *us!*)

You know how faithful she always was, running to meet us after school, tagging us places, challenging anybody she thought might harm us. Oh, God, thank you for her—and forgive me for the times I failed her.

The times I forgot to feed her or was too lazy to walk her even when she begged. The times when she messed up my room or upset the trash and I was so cross to her. My heart breaks to think of it; the tears roll down my cheeks.

Please let her know I'm sorry.

She strives feebly with her paw and I hold it tighter, gaze into her poor pleading eyes. Her tail moves a little and I think she's trying to tell me something . . .

Oh, God, how sad to be dumb, unable to speak, to say words of forgiveness or love. Or even one word—"*Good-by.*"

Where is she going, God? Do pets have souls like us?

Dogs, so eager to please, so loving, so loyal—do you have a place for them somewhere out there among the stars? A place where they can run and bark to their hearts' content, and love again—maybe love the angels? She never really cared about anybody but us, Lord, but don't let her get too lonesome. Don't let her miss us too much.

Please, Lord, if it's in your scheme at all, take care of her for us. And when the rest of us arrive, let her come bounding to meet us.

## THE SHOPPING TRIP

It was a hard fight but we made it, Lord, this shopping trip with my mother.

There were times when I almost had her in tears, times when she almost had *me* in tears. But we finally settled on a few things I liked and she could stand (and pay for), and then took time out for a milkshake.

After that everything looked better. We even got to laughing and wound up friends again.

Forgive me for giving her such a hard time; please make me nicer next time. Thank you (as well as her) for the things she bought me.

And when I have a daughter to take shopping, help me to be as good a sport about it as my mother.

## I'M GLAD I HAVE A BROTHER

I'm glad you gave me a brother, God. Even though I sometimes think he can't stand me. Even when he ignores me, or makes fun of me, or tries to boss me.

I don't know which is worse—when he acts as if I'm poison, hopeless, impossible. Or the times when he tries to improve me. Or when he orders me around—"Wash this shirt, make me a sandwich—"

Furious as he makes me, I'm still glad I have a brother.

A brother to walk with sometimes. To point out to other people and be proud of. To turn to when I've got a problem worthy of his attention. A problem only a guy his age, with his experience, would know how to advise me about.

Thank you for my brother.

And please make me the kind of sister he really likes, even if he doesn't show it. Somebody he's a little bit proud of too, inside. A person he will want to talk to of his own free will sometime.

And someday make me a woman he'll respect and enjoy and even admire. Make him glad he has me for a sister.

## IT'S FUNNY ABOUT FAMILIES

It's funny about families, God.

How we have no choice about them. We're just dropped into one and that's it, take it or leave it. (Only you can't leave it!) Whether or not we like the people in it, whether they're a lot like us or so different we all seem strangers, they're *ours*. We're supposed to love each other and be loyal to each other.

And the funny thing is, we do! In spite of all our differences, we do.

I'm almost ashamed to admit it, but I'm always seeing families I think are superior to mine. I look at richer, more impressive mothers and fathers. People I secretly wish were my parents. I see girls who'd be more fun to live with, I think, than my sisters. And guys—plenty of guys who'd be an improvement on my brothers . . .

Then I feel shocked. The very idea of trading off one of

my own for anybody else is horrifying. Blood *is* thicker than water.

And no matter how we fight among ourselves, let anybody else say one word against us, and look out! My brother might not speak to me for a week, but I know he'd fight for me in a minute. My parents might yell at me—but just let anybody else try it.

We are all behind each other, no matter what. We suffer for each other, and nearly bust with pride in each other.

I guess you gave us families for protection, God. You gave us this group to belong to. People who may or may not understand us, but who are somehow a vital part of us. People who really want the best for us.

This is pretty wonderful, God.

## THE GLORIOUS BIRTHDAY

It's been a glorious birthday, God. Not quite as exciting as when I was little, but still fun.

To wake up with the colored balloons hanging from the ceiling as always, the gaily wrapped packages on the bed. And the family singing "Happy Birthday" with their own crazy lyrics. And tonight some of my friends for dinner, and other kids running in and out, and neighbors too to share the cake and help blow out the candles.

And the flowers from my boy friend, the cards and presents—even my kid brother spending all that money he'd saved from his paper route!

And just sitting around talking and laughing and showing home movies. I hadn't thought I'd want to see them or have my boy friend see them. Me as a bawling baby, or in third grade with my glasses and that toothless grin! . . . But it was really a riot; we laughed until we cried . . .

And then the pictures of our family picnics, our camping trips, and Christmases . . .

I'd looked forward to this birthday, Lord. Not for the celebration but because it meant I'd be another year older. Another year nearer independence, being my own boss, leaving home.

Now, tonight, I'm not so eager to go. This birthday has made me appreciate my family. In spite of our problems we've had wonderful times together, we mean a lot to each other. I feel so lucky that I have them.

Thank you for my wonderful home. Thank you for my family.

# THE BIG SCENE

✾✾✾✾✾✾✾✾

## WHY ARE THEY SO SUSPICIOUS?

Why are adults so suspicious of us, God? Even when we're not doing anything wrong.

These two guys I know were just walking along looking in store windows the other night. Looking at sporting equipment, boots and knives and guns, hunting guns. And they were arguing because there was a stuffed pheasant in the window; and the one who wants to be an ornithologist was admiring it and saying how cruel it was to kill anything so beautiful, or even to kill at all.

And the other kid, who likes to hunt, was kidding him about it and arguing with him.

They weren't doing any harm at all. And yet these two cops came along and ordered them to move on.

Like they expected them to break the window and steal the guns or something. Like maybe they expected them to use the guns if they did—to stick up a bank or a liquor store, at that!

And the boys were angry and humiliated, Lord, moving on. They didn't dare linger even to look in other windows. It gave them a grudge against policeman they hadn't had.

And even though I don't blame them, that's not fair either. Because policemen are just people hired to do a job. There *are* a lot of break-ins and holdups, and it's a dangerous, thankless, often dirty job.

Yet why were these kids automatically under suspicion just because they're teen-agers and their hair is long? Why didn't the officers say, "Hi," and visit with them a few minutes?

They'd have found out why they were hanging around that window—just arguing about a *pheasant,* and the right to kill it!

Lord, please give adults—all adults, parents and policemen—some of the trust and common sense they preach to us. Don't let them be so suspicious of us, God.

## THE SHOPLIFTERS

All this shoplifting, God. What should I do about it? What *can* I do? I'm scared, scared for my friends and scared for myself. I haven't taken anything yet, but I'm afraid I might.

Because everybody's taking stuff. Practically everybody. Kids who've got everything. Kids who don't need it, don't know what to do with it. These girls in one of the best clubs brag about it and have a kind of Show and Tell of the stuff they heist.

I was shocked when I heard about it—and then it seemed kind of cute. And today I was tempted, myself. I was along when one of these girls lifted some false eyelashes.

I was worried, I begged her not to, but all the time my heart was pounding and I wanted to take something myself, just to prove I could. And the excitement of getting out of the place without being caught was awful . . . and thrilling. I'm ashamed to admit it now, but it was. I've got to level with you, God—it was!

Please forgive me and stand by me. Help me to remember it's stealing. I'd be a thief. I don't want to get my thrills by being a thief. A petty thief. Or any kind of thief.

Keep me honest, God.

## TOO PRECIOUS TO SELL

They call this girl "The Body," God. And she's stacked, she really is.

But I've been thinking about these girls that make a big show about simply having—bodies. After all, everybody's got one. And if that's all somebody's got—I mean if that's the whole deal, it's kind of funny and kind of sad.

And to put a body up for sale, Lord. Like topless dancers or the foldouts in magazines. And worse. Girls who pose for lewd pictures for guys to get excited over . . .

To use it for *that,* your own body. Your own private personal body!

You know I'm not a prude, God. I want to be proud of my body, and when the time comes I want to share it.

But the very idea of having it exposed—pawed over, drooled on, used, if only in men's minds. To have it laughed and joked about . . . is just too horrible.

I could cry. I could cry for those girls.

They are insulting and damaging themselves. They are violating themselves. Please help them, God.

## THEY'RE PUTTING ON THE PRESSURE

Help me, Lord, please help me. I'm not as strong as I thought I was, not as well armed against temptation. Especially when the kids include me, kids I've always thought I wanted to be with.

You know how I hate to be left out. And now they're inviting me, acting as if they want me, putting on the pressure. And I feel like such a coward not doing what they do, I feel like such a square.

And I'm curious too. There's this terrible curiosity to know what it's like to get high, whether from drugs or drink or pot. To just go blasting out of myself, get away from it all—responsibilities and problems.

It's glorious, they claim; they have fantastic experiences. They're urging me to try it.

And I'm tempted, Lord. Sometimes almost unbearably tempted.

Please hang onto me, God, don't let me yield.

Because I know it's not always so glorious, and some of the fantastic experiences also lead to hell. Some of these kids are already there, and others are on their way. And it's no fun in hell even if all your friends are there!

Don't let me follow them, Lord. And rescue them too. Lead us all back from hell.

## DELIVER US

Thank you, God, that drugs are on their way out. At least I pray they're on their way out. We've seen what they've done to the older kids. The horrible things drugs do to them and make them do; we've seen their lives ruined. Or ended! And kids our own age too—and even younger ones.

A lot of us are scared, God. Scared and mad and disgusted. It's all so senseless—like playing with dynamite or devils. It's all so *insane!*

It's like the demons they talk about in the Bible. Demons that possessed people and had to be cast out. Drugs must be demons, God. They possess people, literally possess them, and sometimes there seems no way to cast them out.

Only you can help it seems, that's why I'm praying for this boy.

I liked him so much, Lord . . . He was cute and popular. I heard he was smoking pot, but that didn't seem too bad. Then that he was dropping acid. At first I couldn't believe it (he'd have more sense, he'd know it wasn't smart any more), but it's true. He's different, he's sleepy and horrible.

I could cry when I see him, I get so heartsick . . . And now they say he's pushing it, especially on younger kids.

Please don't let him. Oh, God, stop him. Cast out the demon that's possessing him. Order it to leave him!

And please, oh please, drive off every last demon of these drugs that have been tormenting us.

## THE BAD TRIP

My friend's in the hospital, Lord, from a bad trip. A terrible trip.

Don't let her die, don't let her mind be blown altogether. Please bring her back from this awful experience sane and whole again. The way she was before she got started, the wonderful girl she was.

You know she's not a bad girl, God; she didn't do it very often, she wasn't even hooked. She just did it once too often. And now unless you help her she might die, or never be normal again, from this terrible trip.

Save her, God. I must have faith that you will save her. Save her, spare her, and forgive her. And love her, Lord, oh love her. And let her parents keep on loving her.

And her friends. All of us. She's going to need an awful lot of love when she makes it back from this terrible trip.

## WHY DO YOU LET IT HAPPEN?

Evil, Lord, all this evil and suffering.

Why don't you stop it? Sometimes when I hear about things like this, this awful thing that happened, I am so horrified I turn against you.

How could you? I demand. How could a loving God *let it happen?*

Then I realize, I've simply got to realize, that there is evil in the world as well as good. And the evil is powerful too. And if I start blaming you for the evil, running away from you because of the evil, then I'm joining the evil forces too in a way.

Because people who love God don't do the evil things. There wouldn't *be* so much cruelty and evil and suffering if so many people hadn't turned away from you.

It's something like that, Lord. People a lot older and smarter than I am haven't been able to figure it out—how if you really care about us you could allow such tragedies. And because they can't, a lot of them deny you, and live their whole lives without you.

I don't want to be like that, Lord. But this is a choice I've got to make. Either I've got to accept the fact of suffering and evil and go right on loving and trusting you, or I can blame you for them, and live an empty, hopeless, meaningless life without you.

I choose you, God. I believe that the only way I can do anything about all these terrible things is by staying close to you.

## AND THE FIRST STAR PROMISED "TOMORROW!"

Sometimes your world seems so beautiful, Lord, I want to live forever. But sometimes it's so terrible I think I just can't take it.

All the pressures, at home and at school. All the problems, all the pain—not only mine but the suffering everywhere. Wars and crime and cancer and poverty . . . And my own hurts, the bitter personal things that happen to me.

I sometimes think life's just not worth it. I think about dropping out. I have these blind desperate daydreams about it, how to do it. I see it all dramatized, the shock, the headlines. Mainly how people would miss me, how sorry they'd be.

Then I recoil at the conceit of that. For anybody to think he matters that much! The world doesn't stop just because somebody gets off. The kids could go from my funeral to a dance; the guy I love would find somebody else.

Sure, the *shock* would be real (at least for a week, maybe two). And some grief would last forever. (I've seen parents' faces when this happens, God, and it's pretty terrible—I couldn't do that to anybody.)

So I know suicide's not only selfish, it's phony. After all, how phony can you get? To bleed about the world's suffering and then deliberately add to it.

And what happens to people who take their own lives, God?

Do they simply vanish like smoke? . . . Nothing . . . nothing any more, ever. No more hopes, dreams, excitements, loves, or even the troubles they think they can't stand . . . Just blankness, darkness . . . It's too ghastly even to try to imagine . . . to stop *being.*

Or do they really get out of anything? Do they only trade one bag of agony for something worse?

To fling your most precious creation back into your face. A human life. A body. A living breathing body. To throw it all away, throw it back into your face . . . !

I know you love us, I know you forgive us. I know you understand what we have to go through. But that. To do *that* . . . Well, it must cause you great suffering too.

Dear God, don't let me ever cause such suffering even by thinking of it. Forgive me such thoughts.

And whenever they come back, help me to remember this:

Suicide is selfish.
Suicide is phony.
Suicide is cruel.
Suicides are quickly forgotten.
If other people can take it, so can I.
If other people can rejoice in life, so can I.

And let me remember this:

The glorious days I wouldn't want to have missed . . . A day when I was working hard on something I enjoyed . . . A day when I got good news . . . A day when somebody gave me something I always wanted . . . A day when I was in love . . .

A day when the house was warm after a freezing walk, and supper tasted good . . . A day when the sunset lingered and the first star promised, *"Tomorrow!"*

## SUNRISE AND SINGING

Sunrise, God, and singing . . . high on this mountaintop.

The birds are singing, the kids are singing, and it's as if our voices are driving away the gray, it's going fast, the pink glow is claiming the sky as we sing on your mountaintop.

And the sun is listening to us, its scarlet face is beginning to peer over the mountain, as if we've raised it by our singing. And we greet it with a shout of triumph, a glory shout!

But even in this joy of sunrise and singing, God, I'm thinking of the kids who couldn't come. Who wouldn't or couldn't come. Still down there in bed, gray with anguish too many of them, grabbing at life yet missing life, missing the mountain.

The leader is praying now, thanking you for this day, this sparkling air, and my heart joins in. . . Thank you for the little stream that dances as if to our singing . . . and the crackling of the bright fire frying our bacon, and the smell of the coffee boiling and the tang of the tall pine forest.

Thank you, oh thank you, that I'm here to enjoy all this, high with the sheer beauty of the morning and my friends, and feeling close to you.

But I can't forget them, God, the kids down there.

They're trying to find something too. Some excitement, some vision, some meaning. Only they think we're suckers to climb for it, they think there are shortcuts, they want to be carried.

Bless them, Lord, and wake them up, wash the gray sickness out of them, open their eyes, their ears.

Maybe by some miracle you can make them hear us singing even now! Calling to them to join us, come with us. Be willing to climb the mountain.

## IT'S GOT TO BEGIN AT HOME

I keep wondering about world peace, Lord.

It seems so *simple*. If all the young people in all the countries would just say, "This is too crazy, we won't fight your rotten wars."

And if all the older people who are making them would just stop being so selfish and decide to get along.

Then I think of this family and the fighting that goes on. The conflicts between Dad and my brothers, Mother and us girls. And the kids themselves, fighting with each other. Everybody wanting his own way, everybody protecting what he's got and wanting a little more.

Sure, lots of times sharing, having fun and sticking by each other. Even drawing up peace pacts and non-aggression pacts. Only even these unwritten alliances don't last very long.

So maybe all the greed and selfishness we find in families is just blown up on a larger scale in wars. No wonder whole nations fight each other! Nations are just a lot of people like us who've been used to fighting for every little thing at home.

How can we expect world peace if we can't even get along with our own families in the same house?

Every single person alive yelling "Peace!" has got to start with himself. He's just as bad as the worst warmonger if he can't stop fighting with the people he knows.

And this means me. And I'm going to need your help.

We all are going to need your help. Thank you for that help, God.

## THE BIG SCENE

It's a big scene out there, God. The world's a great big worrisome scene where an awful lot is wrong.

Part of me is scared of it, God, part doesn't want to be bothered. "Pay no attention," part of me says, "you'll have enough just learning how to be happy." But I know I'll never be really happy unless I at least try to make it better.

I can't go my own merry way blind to other people's needs.

Poor people and sick people, and people society has given a raw deal. The fact that I'm so lucky is all the more reason—I've got to do something to help them. Maybe help change the whole picture.

But how, Lord, how?

I know that strikes and riots and tearing things down is no way. We kids have been through all that. The leaders never had any answers, none that work anyway—only big mouths and a desire for power. They hurt more people than they helped.

I don't want to destroy things, God, I want to *build.*

And I'm beginning to realize how long it takes. So give me patience. Help me remember there's no such thing as an instant cure for the world's ills. Instant equality for everybody, or instant peace.

My parents tell me they found that out—they too were going to reform the world! It's so easy to blame them for the mess, but they really tried. And though they failed in some ways, in others they made progress.

Help me to recognize that progress, and to remember that it took time. Please don't let me get discouraged before I start, God. Keep my hopes and enthusiasm high.

As for now, show me how to get ready, where to begin.

The first thing, surely, is to get my education. Without that I won't be much good to anybody, even myself. But I can practice too. Thank you that there are so many places where I can start to serve.

Like this volunteer job I've just taken on at the Home for Incurables. It's pretty grim there, God, but if I can't give up a few hours a week to help some hopeless people then

I've got no right to weep over the world's misery. No right to criticize.

Thank you for this opportunity, and others that will come. Guide me to the right ones, God, and guide my friends.

For all our faults, kids today are really concerned. We want to get involved. We don't want happiness only for ourselves; we also want it for our fellow men.

# I WANT
# TO BE ME

## I WANT TO BE ME

I'm sick of trying to be a lot of people I'm not, Lord. Or even just one other person I'm not.

My parents are always trying to make me over. Why can't I be like my cousin, or the president of the class, or even (heaven forbid) like Mom when she was a girl?

Teachers try to make me over—I've got to be this way or that way if I want to be successful, get the kind of job I should, get into a certain college.

Even my friends try to make me into somebody else. Laugh like them, walk and talk and act like them, dress like them, think like them. If I don't I'm a freak, or worse —square.

Even the freaks and squares try to make me over. I've got to be as way-out as they are, or a squarer square. I'm expected to conform even to the nonconformists.

Lord, I don't want to be anybody else.

Not my parents.
Not my teachers.
Not my friends.

Not even somebody I've read about or seen in the movies or on TV. I know we can learn a lot from other people, pick up all sorts of tricks and improvements from them. But outside and inside too where it really counts I'd rather be myself.

Whoever that is. I'm not sure yet but I'm trying to find out. And if I keep trying to be all these other people, I never will.

Please help me to find and be true to myself, Lord. The person you meant me to be.

## FAITH IN MYSELF

God give me faith in myself.

Not only on the days when I'm going great and winning and nothing seems impossible . . . but on days when the whole world looks lousy and I'm losing and the road ahead seems too hard. When I wonder if I'm brave enough, smart enough, strong enough, and I must be crazy to try.

Don't let me quit, Lord, not ever. Let me keep faith in myself.

No matter how many people discourage me, doubt me, laugh at me, warn me, think me a fool—don't let me listen, Lord. Let me hear another voice telling me, "You can do it, and you will!"

If nobody else in this whole world gives a darn or believes in me, let me believe in myself.

I know there'll be times when I fail. Lord, don't let my failures throw me, don't let them weaken my faith. Let them only make it stronger. Let me believe in myself.

I know there'll be times when I doubt my own ability, when I'll be discouraged, on the verge of despair. Don't let me give up; hang onto me. Fan the fires of my faith so that I'll try even harder. Give me even more faith in myself.

You are the source of life and power and me. You are the source of my abilities—and my faith. Thank you that I can turn to you for reinforcements. That you will give me what I ask—faith in myself.

## WORDS

I come to you ashamed, Lord. Forgive me my dirty mouth.

I used to hate talk like I've just been using, but I hear so much of it I guess I don't mind any more. And this weekend with these kids I don't feel quite secure with, kids I wanted to impress, I was amazed at what came out.

You should have heard me! (Well, I guess you did.)

And now I wish you hadn't; wish I hadn't heard myself. I felt proud of myself at the time, but now I feel . . . kind of sick.

Sure, a word is a word, lots of people say. We've even got a teacher who claims there are no "bad words" at all. A word can't hurt you, use any word you want any old time.

But I'm confused about this, Lord. Please help me figure it out. If there are good words, words to express love and beauty, then there must be some bad words too. Words to curse with, hate with, foul things up with.

If not, if all words were the same, without any meaning, then how could any of us ever say anything? How could we express anything? Especially how we feel. How could we be understood?

Is the teacher right, Lord? Is a curse as good as a blessing? Are the words little kids write on walls and big kids use to make ourselves feel bigger, as pleasant and charming as anything in the dictionary?

As I talk to you about this, I think I'm getting my answer.

Some words *can* hurt us. There are some words I couldn't use around anyone I really respected, or that I wanted to respect me. The wife of the President, for instance. Or somebody big in a college I wanted to get into.

Or a boy I really cared about.

Or you. No, I couldn't swear or use those words in talking to you.

Language is so marvelous, Lord! We have such a wide wonderful choice of words. Let me learn lots of them.

Don't let me use the bad ones because I don't know enough good ones. Or because I feel I've got to show off.

## I'M SO IMPATIENT

I'm so impatient, Lord.

Impatient with people, impatient with myself. Even impatient with life.

My dreams are so urgent, so vivid, so real. I want them to happen *now*. I can hardly bear the thought of years more school. (Sometimes I can hardly bear the thought of another day!) Years of being bossed, nagged, advised, of having to take orders.

I want to get going. I want to get out, start making my own decisions, living my own life. I want to be free.

This impatience, Lord—it sometimes threatens to explode. I get wild notions of doing like some kids, just dropping everything, taking off. But then I see what happens to the ones who do. My girl friends who ran away and got married—it looked so romantic, but now they're tied down worse than before.

And the ones who've gone the drug route—it's too terrible what's happening to so many of them. Lost, missing, in courts or jails or hospitals, their minds smashed, their lives ruined, maybe forever.

Impatience is to blame for a lot of this, Lord. Sheer intolerable impatience. They couldn't wait, as I think sometimes I can't wait. They wanted life to be a Happening, instead of just happening, boringly predictable day after day.

God, give all of us more patience.

Keep us on course, don't let us go plunging blindly down shortcuts that only lead no place. Or that in the end mean time lost, years lost, and a fight back that will take twice as long.

Please, God, give me patience.

## DEEP TROUBLE

I'm in trouble, Lord, deep trouble, and I don't know what to do.

I'm afraid to tell my folks. It would break their hearts. I don't think they could possibly understand. And if they turn against me now, if they blame and berate me, I don't think I can stand it. (I've already blamed myself, I've already punished myself.)

Yet my friends aren't much help—they've got troubles enough of their own. And I can't think who else to turn to.

Oh, God, guide me to somebody who will understand. Or give me the courage to go to my parents, and please, please make them understand.

Right now I've got to have somebody who'll help me instead of lecture me. Who will forgive me, who will not only help me solve this problem but give me back my self-respect.

Thank you for *your* forgiveness and understanding, God. I know that if I just keep close to you, you will lead me out of this deep trouble.

## TALENTS

Thank you for the talents you've given me, God. Don't let me waste them, throw them away on wrong things; don't let me bury them.

I've been thinking about that story in the Bible. The parable of the guy who tested his servants by giving each of them some talents. And the ones who went out and did something with their talents were rewarded when he got back. He gave them more. But one of them, the dummy, just buried his. So in the end he lost it. His master took it away and gave it to somebody else!

There must be so many buried talents, Lord.

My mother's friend, always bragging about what a great voice she used to have—only now she can't sing much better than anybody else. And other people, too, saying how if they'd only gone on with their art or modeling or whatever it was . . .

Only they didn't. Their talents got buried in something. Doubts maybe? Or an easier way to get ahead? Or maybe just plain everyday living. Anyway, they're gone now. And I wonder . . .

I wonder if they dried up and vanished. Or if maybe they were taken—somehow taken and given to the people who already had some talents and were using them. So that they had more!

Anyway, I want to use my talents, Lord. I've got to use them—train and study and practice and polish them. So that they won't go to waste and be an insult to you who gave them to me. And so that they'll do for me and for the world what you meant them to.

God, I'm beginning to see that it's a great responsibility to have talents. Or even just one talent. A responsibility to you.

And if it hurts you to see your gifts buried, going to waste, it must hurt you even more to see them used for wrong! Used not to help but to damage other people. Used for ugliness instead of beauty, to destroy instead of build.

Evil has a big demand for talent too, and I hear the pay is great.

Lord, don't let me hoard my talents, let me make the most of them. But always for good and to your glory.

I am so grateful for my talents, God.

## THIS WONDERFUL BODY

Thank you for this wonderful body.

I want it to be a beautiful body so badly. Right now I'm kind of sway-backed, and I'm too big some places and not as big as I'd like to be other places, but it's coming. It's got real possibilities, God.

And it can do so many things! Swim, dance, skate, ride. Not as expertly as I want to, but if I practice and take care of my body I can do them better, and more. I want to learn to ski and skin-dive—oh, Lord, I want to do so many things.

And I want to love someone very much with my body, and to bear children with strong healthy bodies, beautiful bodies.

And oh, I want to keep my body beautiful always, the way it is now—or is going to be!

But life does such awful things to bodies, God. I dread to think of it, I shudder to see them. So many women who once were girls themselves, excited about their bodies, lovely blooming bodies, now gotten fat and dumpy. Or shriveled and stiff and slouched.

Why does this happen, Lord? Does it have to happen? Or do people just *let* it happen?

I know we can't be Miss Americas all our lives; I know it's easy when you're young to say, "I'll never get old!" But oh, God, don't let me ever stop caring about my body. Don't let me get lazy or indifferent to how it looks and acts.

With your help I *won't* turn into a fat lady gobbling peanuts and candy at a bridge table, or guzzling drinks at a country club. I won't be a wheezing, coughing, chain-smoking hag.

And I read someplace that the only reason people can't do things as they get older is because they stop doing them. So I don't have to let my body get stiff and stodgy and unable to do the things I love now. Not if I keep on doing them.

Lord, I realize life gets complicated and it's not always easy to do what we know is best for us. But surely what we want to do *enough,* we can.

Please, God, give me a beautiful body, and the desire and the will power to keep it all my life.

## THE SECRET PLACE

There is a secret place in me, there is a small secret place that must be the resting place of my soul.

I want to keep certain things there that I don't tell anyone else except you about. Things all for myself to remember, all for myself to consider, all for myself to think about.

A few experiences that are special, a few problems and pains and humiliations too terrible and yet wonderfully a part of myself, or even just too awful to reveal.

And a few special dreams, a few special plans.

Only you can really share these with me, God, because you made me in the beginning and created this private little core of me.

I have no secrets from you, I can keep no secrets from you.

Thank you for giving me this private place where nobody else can enter, this little chapel of myself.

## IT'S SO GLORIOUS TO BE ALIVE

Oh, God, it's so glorious to be alive sometimes!

I don't know why, but there are days when I feel so in love with everybody. Not just one special boy, but all boys, and all the girls too. In spite of our rivalry and picking at each other, some days they just seem so dear, so sweet, so funny, so much a part of me.

On such days I love my own family in a new way, for all their faults; I even love my teachers.

I guess you'd say I'm just in love with life.

To be alive, Lord—just to be alive. It's so wonderful sometimes it almost hurts.

Just to bite into an apple and really taste it, tangy and juicy on my tongue . . . To run the dog and feel the wind slamming us along, or the rain cold on my face . . . Or to just lie baking in the hot golden sun.

Or to dance until I drip . . . or dive into bitter-cold water and swim . . . Or to feel the horse beneath me as we soar over a jump.

My own body is sometimes suddenly so marvelous to me! I'm somehow in love with it too, because it can do so many things, enjoy so many things, *feel* so many things.

And my mind, God—the mystery of my own mind.

My mind with its ability to learn, to create, to comprehend. My mind with all its exciting thoughts.

It's almost too amazing, that you gave me not only this incredible body but this secret yet powerful thing, my mind!

On some days the rest of my life stretches before me with such promise, Lord, such shining promise.

Nothing is impossible, I can do anything I really want to do. I can be successful. I can be rich and famous if I want. I can love and marry a terrific man.

But above all, I can make some gift to this world you have let me enter. I must be here for some purpose, and that purpose will be revealed to me. Anyway, I *must* do something for it, if only to repay you for letting me be born in the first place.

It's so glorious to be alive, Lord. Thank you for creating me.

# YOU ARE WITH ME

## YOU ARE WITH ME

How good it is to know I can talk to you, God, wherever I am, whatever I do.

You are with me always. In a classroom, at a football game, on a date. No place is too high for you to be with me, no place too earthy or common.

You are with me walking onto a platform to make a speech—I can whisper my inmost pleas to you even there. You are with me bathing and dressing or cleaning my room.

I needn't wait to go to church to worship you. I needn't wait for a special time and place to cry out to you for help, or to thank you, or pour out my heart to you.

You are with me in crowds of people, you are with me when I'm alone (oh, sometimes so desperately alone).

Friends so often fail me. Parents aren't always there. The world of people can't possibly know or care what becomes of me; they can't understand, they can't be expected to share. Only you, who made each of us, are a part of us in this remarkable way.

You breathe with us, think with us, feel with us. So we needn't be afraid to say, "Okay, you're along for the trip!"

So often such a rough trip, God; so often a glorious and gay one.

Yet just knowing that you're always available for the asking, here with me to help me just for the asking . . . it's almost too wonderful sometimes to realize.

## WHEN WE'RE YOUNG YOU ESPECIALLY UNDERSTAND

I know that you are with us, God. That you suffer when we suffer, are happy when we're happy, love when we love.

You aren't blind and cold and indifferent to what happens to us.

But you don't hate when we hate, and you don't sin when we sin. Instead of hating, you love us and forgive us. And the sin hurts you because you know it hurts us.

But you forgive us that too, and give us another chance.

And you understand, you do understand.

I think when we are young and trying to find our way, you especially understand.

## WHY DO THEY MAKE IT SO COMPLICATED?

Why do so many churches make religion so complicated, God? And so fancy. And get so far away from the things you sent Jesus to teach us.

Jesus was a simple guy like us. And what he taught was simple: To love each other, to heal and help each other. To forgive each other and love even our enemies. To live simply too, and not worry about tomorrow.

Hard, sure, some of it very hard. But simple, that's the main thing. And he said it in plain, everyday language.

So I don't see why so many churches make it so complicated or so fancy. (Lots of preachers even *talk* fancy in solemn quavering ham-acty voices I know he'd never use!) Or why they spend millions of dollars on fancy buildings while people go hungry.

Jesus taught us to feed the poor, not make the rich more comfortable on Sunday. He taught us to clothe the naked and heal the sick.

I know churches do these things too, but I sure don't think he ever expected them to sock away billions in investments and businesses, not as long as there was one person cold or hungry or crippled.

He said we should "take no thought for tomorrow." That's a laugh. Some churches don't think about much else.

Above all, he said you want us to love each other. Yet some churches are full of hate. They fight among themselves. Or they attack other churches, whole churches attack other churches.

And some churches talk more about politics and social issues than they do about you, God. Or they go the other way and hammer and yell and preach as if nothing's happened in the world since Noah built the ark. When what we're really hungry for is simply—you. A place to learn more about you. Your power, your love, how you are with us all the time and can help us cope with life today.

These are some of the reasons a lot of people don't go to church any more, God. It's not that they don't love you, it's just that they don't find you there. Not in too many churches.

Some churches don't draw people closer to you, they get between.

And a lot of people don't know there's any other kind.

## SOMETIMES I HATE GOING TO CHURCH

Sometimes I hate going to church, Lord.

It's just too much trouble sometimes, getting up and getting ready, especially if I've been up late the night before.

But if I make myself go I'm usually glad. Just to be up and out in the bright morning, with the church bells ringing and calling. And the people glad to see me when I get there, and the people I'm glad to see. Usually the more I dread it the gladder I am I came.

Sometimes the sermon is dull, the music downright depressing. But I can enjoy the *place* . . . the flowers on the altar, the light rainbowing through the windows, the look, the feel of a special place designed for the purpose of worshiping you.

And I can enjoy my thoughts. If my mind wanders I'm sure you forgive me. A church is one place where a person can *have* a little quiet and peace in which to dream . . . Or I can read the stuff in the Bible (such marvelous stuff, so much of it). I can read the Psalms. They never let you down, those Psalms.

(Anyway I don't go to church to be *entertained!*)

But usually it's not like that. The songs are lively, or they have something special to say to me. The leaders are young and vital in our church, the assistant is with it, he speaks our language.

And the whole place is waking up, trying new things. Some of the older people object, some throw up their hands in horror, but most of them are good sports about it. Some of them even like it, they were fed up with the staleness of some of the same old ways.

Anyway, Lord, it's worth it.

Worth the effort, just being with other people who want to be with other people and with you.

I always get something out of it, even if I have to *make* something out of it. Thanks for making me go, God, on those days when I don't want to.

## THIS WAS CHURCH FOR ME

Thank you, God, for this service. This beautiful, moving service that they let us have.

We wrote our own songs and sang them, to the accompaniment of guitars. One of the guys preached the sermon, only it didn't sound like a sermon, it was just a talk about life and us and you; our hopes and our hangups—how you can help. We were free to join in.

And then we had Communion, with a big loaf of bread and a jug of wine.

Another girl served the Sacraments. She blessed the bread and broke it. She poured the wine. (She was as reverent and giving as any minister, any man.)

Two of the guys were assistants. And it couldn't have been any more precious from the hands of ministers. They *were* your ministers, Lord, even if they hadn't gone to seminary and studied and learned the rules. The only rules they followed were those given at the Last Supper: "Do this in remembrance of me."

And we remembered, we remembered! Remembered in a way that will last.

Then we followed another commandment that was given at that same time: "Love one another."

We all turned around and embraced each other, we walked around hugging and kissing each other and speaking words of joy, words of comfort, words of love. Age didn't matter, skin color didn't matter, how we were dressed didn't matter. All that mattered was that we were together, *your* children, your family, loving one another and not afraid to say so. Not afraid to keep that command.

And we left still loving each other and life and you. Wanting to help, wanting to share—share everything we have. And to find more people to share that shining love with. People who are lost and lonely, or in trouble and needing love so bad.

That was church, Lord. Thank you for it. That was truly church for me.

## DON'T LET ME EVER LOSE YOU

Go with me, God, go with me. Don't let me ever lose you.

Sometimes I feel so close to you; sometimes I don't. But when you're gone there's something missing. I'm empty, I'm insecure.

I may think I'm happy but I'm not, not really. I don't like other people as much, don't like myself as much. And I don't feel really safe.

Life sometimes gets between us, God. People get between us. Temptations and things I'm uneasy about and ashamed of get between us.

But please don't abandon me. Draw me always back to you. Don't ever let me lose you altogether.

## IS THIS WHY BLESSINGS WORK?

I've been thinking some more about blessings, Lord. Wondering why they work.

It must be because thoughts are so strong. In some ways the strongest thing in the world. Like electricity or TV waves; we can't see them, but they're there.

And the Bible tells us (and psychologists too) that what we think, we are. What we think, we become. Our thoughts can even hurt or help to heal our bodies. And sometimes the bodies of other people too.

Jesus healed people just by thinking about them sometimes. And he said if we believed, we too could do these wonders.

This helps me to understand the strange power of blessings. Because if thoughts are all that strong, we ought to use them to help each other. There is so much evil in the world there must be unseen evil in the air—hate and resentment that we can combat with thoughts of love.

Blessings are thoughts of love. And the glorious thing is, we never run out. The more often we remember to use them the more love we have to give. And the better we feel.

Whenever I bless somebody else, I'm receiving a blessing too!

Even if I don't understand all about why blessings work, I know that much at least. Thank you for being the source of blessing, God.

## THE COURAGE AND THE TRUTH

Jesus spoke the truth when he lived here as one of us. He wasn't afraid to be honest; he didn't compromise with anybody; he didn't tone things down.

I wish I had that kind of confidence, that courage. I've got to compromise lots of times, Lord. I don't always dare to say what I think, what I believe (lots of times I don't even *know*). But when I fail you, please make allowances.

Jesus knew who he was, where he came from and why he was here. I don't know who I am or the real purpose of my life yet. But I am trying to find out.

And I want to be like him, to have that kind of courage. To not be afraid to walk with the outcasts and help those who need me. Nor afraid to be honest, stand up for what I believe.

To suffer, if I have to, for what I believe. Even be willing to die for what I believe.

Please guide me to the real truths, God. And as I find them give me the strength to follow that example, based not only on words but deeds.

## STAY NEAR TO ME

Stay near to me, Lord, keep me near to you, and let me learn to love you more.

I think maybe if I can be close to you now and really love you, then I'll always have you. I won't be so lonely and lost when I'm older. There won't be the awful emptiness in my life I see in so many people.

Women nagging and complaining, or screaming about liberation. Men working too hard, sometimes at jobs they hate. Men taking advantage of the women; all the conflicts between men and women. All the fighting that goes on—whole families fighting. And the escape routes people take, drinking and drugs and cheating on each other.

I shudder to think of this, Lord. I know I'll be a part of the whole scene someday, and it won't be easy, none of it will be easy. But if you are really a part of my life, with me in whatever I do, then I'll always have a friend, a comforter, someone who understands me, someone I can always talk to.

I'll have a source of strength I can depend on, and it will make me a better person, so that other people will be better too.

Stay close to me, Lord. When I neglect you, bring me back.

I need you now, but someday I'll probably need you more. Let my love for you grow even stronger. Keep me always close to you.